BUILDING THE B-29

JACOB VANDER MEULEN

BUILDING THE B-29

SMITHSONIAN INSTITUTION PRESS

WASHINGTON AND LONDON

Copy Editor: Initial Cap Editorial Services

Production Editor: Duke Johns

Designer: Alan Carter

Library of Congress Cataloging-in-Publication Data

Vander Meulen, Jacob.

Building the B-29 / Jacob Vander Meulen.

p.   cm.

Includes bibliographical references.

ISBN 1-56098-609-3 (alk. paper)

1. B-29 bomber—Design and construction—History. 2. World war, 1939–1945—Influence.

3. Aircraft industry—Military aspects—United States—History. I. Title.

TL685.3.V27   1995

623.7'463'0973—dc20   95-8548

British Library Cataloguing-in-Publication Data is available

Manufactured in the United States of America

02 01 00 99 98 97 96 95   5 4 3 2 1

∞ The paper used in this publication meets the minimum requirements of the
American National Standard for Information Sciences—Permanence of Paper for
Printed Library Materials Z39.48-1984.

CONTENTS

Preface   6

Acknowledgments   10

Origins of the B-29   11

Arranging B-29 Production   21

Changes and Painful Delays   30

Why Wichita?   36

Renton and Seattle: "The Big Change"   56

Omaha   69

Marietta, Georgia   74

Who Built the Engines?   86

Conclusion   99

Note on Sources   101

PREFACE

The B-29 Superfortress is one of the most famous and most important warplanes ever built. Many remember its devastating raids in the Korean War but it is better known for the ways Americans used it against Japan during World War II. In 1945, B-29s destroyed large sections of Japanese cities with high explosives and firebombs and dropped atomic bombs on Hiroshima and Nagasaki. *Enola Gay* and *Bocks Car*, the Superfortresses that delivered the only nuclear weapons ever used, are credited with finally bringing World War II to an end in August 1945.

But the B-29's history is important in more than just military terms. It was also a major episode in the ongoing story of how Americans experience rapid changes in technology and industry. Building nearly 4,000 B-29s altered the economic and social life of hundreds of thousands of Americans. It introduced many workers to the industrial life for the first time and changed the way older workers experienced the factory. For engineers, technicians, and business executives it meant their first exposure to large-scale, high-technology military projects.

The B-29 meant new work-a-day worlds across America, especially in the states and regions where Superfortress "factory-nests" were built. Indeed, the flexibility of American workers, the way they quickly adapted to change, made the B-29 program a success. At the same time, the program points to certain patterns of stability in America's political and cultural life. Despite the World War II emergency and the urgency and complications of the B-29 program, Americans barely altered their traditional approach to using government for new problems and challenges.

This book outlines this history in ways that should be interesting for the average reader. Readers should get a good sense of the struggles during the 1930s among different ideas that led to the B-29's development, the many challenges connected with producing it in big numbers, and the project's enormous costs to taxpayers. The story of the B-29 offers a chance to think about the links between war and society in America, between combat fronts and homefronts in a global war like World War II. It provides a glimpse into America's early aircraft industry and its dealings with the federal government. It is a good case study of national industrial policy, of military-industrial relations, and of the unique way government works in America.

The B-29 project was a big part of the military restructuring of the nation's economy during World War II and its rearrangement along regional lines. Massive spending on weapons such as the Superfortress put people to work, generated prosperity, and drew the nation out of the Great Depression's dark days. The project fostered new and advanced industries in depressed parts of rural America, particularly the South and the Great Plains. The four aircraft plants built for the B-29 are, fifty years later, among the most important sites for American airpower and aerospace design and manufacture. They offer many of the nation's most interesting and best-paid jobs.

It is easy to think of a bomber's performance as mainly the work

A B-29 in flight over the Great Plains. The B-29's wingspan measures 141 feet. Its length from nose to tail turret is 99 feet and its tail rises to almost 28 feet. This particular Superfortress was built at the Boeing plant in Wichita, Kansas. Courtesy of the National Air and Space Museum, Smithsonian Institution (5316-7A).

of pilots and crews. Actually, the crew were the end-runners of a great outpouring of national effort, energy, and resources. Building B-29s was one of the biggest and most complicated things Americans ever did. A very large and advanced airplane, the B-29 needed a manufacturing system built basically from scratch. At a cost to taxpayers of roughly three billion 1943 dollars, the B-29 made up the most expensive single part of the overall American weapons-building program for the war.

Hundreds of thousands of Americans built 3,895 B-29s. They worked in four giant new plants in Wichita, Kansas; Marietta, Georgia; Omaha, Nebraska; and Renton, near Seattle in Washington State. They also worked in two huge new engine factories in Woodridge, New Jersey, and in Chicago; at the many factories where B-29 electronic systems and equipment were made; in the hundreds of plants all across the land that did B-29 subcontracting; or in special modification centers and airbases where workers prepared the aircraft to fight.

These people—men and women of all ages—had their lives briefly but intensely transformed by the B-29. Many still have vivid memories of their experiences as young people working in factory and wage-earning roles for the first time. They remember how their cities, towns, and regions were forever altered by the enormous new investment in factories, transportation, and social services, all for the Superfortress.

Some of the most striking aspects of the program are the technical and financial gambles made on the B-29 design and how quickly designers and engineers took each costly step from conception, through research and development, setting up for mass production, organizing a national supply network for parts and materials, and then actual mass production. The process began slowly in 1940 but accelerated into top priority in 1941. Still, as late as mid-1943, no one really knew if the Superfortress would actually work or if there ever would be enough B-29s to make a difference in the war and fill the military's intended ambitions.

To the great relief and delight of everyone involved, the B-29 proved a formidable weapon. By mid-1944 squadrons of Superfortresses were in action on the other side of the planet. In 1945, they devastated the city centers and war economy of Japan and finally convinced Japanese leaders that the war they started was hopeless. Most Americans remain proud of the B-29s and their role in the war against Japan. But many also have misgivings, even regrets, about the violent ways the B-29s were used. Japanese people who died in B-29 raids far outnumber all American soldiers killed in all the fighting theaters of World War II. Still, at the time the attacks seemed fair justice to Americans who knew B-29s were "carpet-bombing," "de-housing," and "incinerating" Japanese cities. They thought Japanese civilians working at war-factory jobs like themselves made fair military targets—whether they were at work or at home, men, women, and children.

Such perplexing issues are not the subject of this book. Instead, it traces the B-29's technical and professional achievements at home and the accomplishments of the American people who

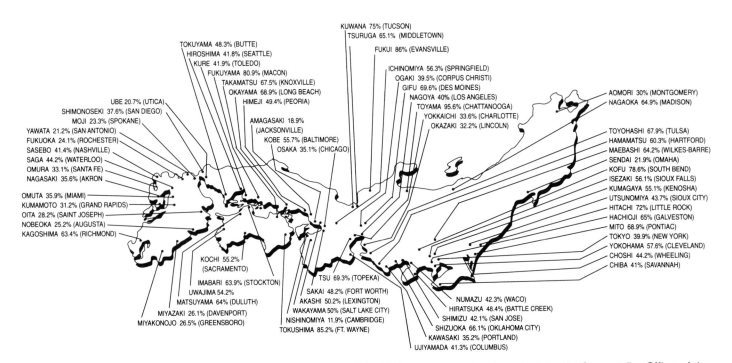

This map of Japan is redrawn from one that appeared as the centerpiece of the 1945 report to the Secretary of War by the Commanding Officer of the U.S. Army Air Forces, Gen. Henry "Hap" Arnold. It was intended to help Americans get a clearer sense of what B-29s did to Japanese cities. The map's original caption reads, "This map of Japan shows the principal industrial cities burned out by B-29 incendiary attacks. Figures indicate what part of the city was destroyed. For comparison, each city is paired with a U.S. city of approximately the same size." Courtesy of the National Air and Space Museum, Smithsonian Institution (AC-59397).

quickly organized themselves and built and made ready large numbers of them. One can't help but be impressed with these successes. The B-29 was a triumph of combined national effort and an unprecedented event in the history of industrial America. The Army officer in charge of a secret 1948 report on the program called it "a giant undertaking" that paid off "in the number of B-29 airplanes that blanketed the skies over Japan." The B-29 program "was by far the largest and most complicated of the several joint production programs undertaken by the Army Air Forces and leading aircraft and automotive companies in this country," he wrote.

Yet the history of the B-29 project is not well known. In 1946, the author of the only other published study of the B-29's production history called it "the most *organizational* airplane ever built. . . . The results achieved shall go down as a monument in the industrial history of this country." The B-29 program shows how a country's social, economic, and cultural makeup shapes the way it organizes and fights. The B-29 reflected the size, wealth, and dynamism of the U.S. economy—the most powerful economy in the world. It reflected the depth of the nation's natural resources—the energy supplies and raw materials, especially aluminum—that were always enough. More important, the B-29 expressed the depth of the nation's human resources—the men and women always there in enough numbers and with the right skills, motivation, and attitudes to design and plan the B-29, build and work the factories, and deal with problems when things didn't go right.

There was nothing inevitable about the B-29 or how it was used in the war. Only Americans could have built an aircraft as powerful as the Superfortress when they did and in so many numbers. Each B-29 recorded the hundreds of thousands of work-hours that went into them. They also reflected the traditional rules Americans followed as they approached the war's social challenges. The B-29 meant a significant new step in the influence of the federal government as it transformed the economic lives of many people. But America's political system and democratic values of individualism and limited government were never in danger, despite the war emergency. Government officials and politicians had little need to coerce the businessmen, managers, and workers who built the B-29. The size and strengths of America's economy and society meant plenty of room for thinking big and for making mistakes, but also for learning from mistakes, for cooperation, initiative, and hard work to undo them and succeed.

ACKNOWLEDGMENTS

This project benefited throughout from the comments, criticisms, and encouragement of staff members at the National Air and Space Museum and the Smithsonian Institution Press, panelists at the 1993 Society for the History of Technology meeting, archivists at the Boeing Company, and Fred Koke, Mark Tamminga, and Eugene Rocca. It depended on grants from the Smithsonian Institution and the Social Sciences and Humanities Research Council of Canada.

ORIGINS OF THE B-29

uilding 3,895 B-29s during World War II involved men and women from all across the country and from many different backgrounds—first-time factory workers, skilled craftsmen and technicians, Army officers and enlisted men, business executives, engineers, scientists, and politicians. But the ideas that led to the B-29 came from just a handful of officers in the Army Air Corps before World War II began.

These officers believed in the concept of strategic bombing. Henry "Hap" Arnold, Frank Andrews, Ira Eaker, Haywood Hansell, A. W. Robins, and Carl Spaatz thought that big airplanes able to carry large loads of bombs over very long distances were essential for American national security. If war came, these planes would fly far behind the frontlines of ground and sea battles and attack "strategic targets," such as the enemy's home-command centers, railroads, energy supplies, and factories. These officers believed that such air attacks would wear down the enemy's morale and ability to fight and thus lead to victory.

When in 1937 Air Corps officers laid out their hopes for a "very long range bomber," the idea of strategic bombing was already more than twenty years old. Since before the First World War, some people had been excited, and others terrified, at how aircraft had changed war. But the potential of strategic bombing was mainly guesswork because aircraft technology was just too primitive to make much of a case for its military uses. In addition, most Americans opposed heavy spending on the military, so the Air Corps and the Navy found it very difficult to get congressmen to provide enough tax money for developing better aircraft.

By the mid-1930s the situation began to change. Americans who were worried about both the possibility of war in Europe and Japanese ambitions in the Far East began supporting the idea of beefing up the military. Meanwhile, aircraft design took some very big steps forward. Metals rather than wood and cloth were utilized in the construction of the fuselage, wings, and tail. Aircraft became much more reliable. They flew through the air much faster and for greater distances because their shapes were better streamlined and because engines had more power.

The design of heavy bombers improved dramatically in 1936 when Boeing's B-17 Flying Fortress first flew. A large metal single-wing plane with four powerful engines and a range of 2,000 miles,

A B-17 Flying Fortress in its late-wartime configuration with more armor, a new chin turret and half-inch guns, staggered waist gunner positions and improved tail turret, all to ward off enemy fighter planes and antiaircraft shells. One of nearly 12,700 produced during World War II by the Boeing, Lockheed, and Douglas companies, this particular "Fort" was built in 1943 at the Boeing plant in Seattle at about the time the B-29 was going into production. Courtesy of the National Air and Space Museum, Smithsonian Institution (AC-28363).

the "Fort" could carry its crew, enough fuel, and a ton of bombs to a target 1,000 miles away and then return to base. The B-17 excited Air Corps officers who believed in strategic bombing, but they realized it would take many more Forts to have any real impact in a possible war.

Unfortunately, there was still plenty of opposition to the idea of strategic bombing. Many officers in the Navy, the Army, even the Air Corps, doubted that strategic bombing could live up to the claims made. These opponents thought it too risky to spend big shares of limited military budgets on unproven heavy bombers, especially when the nation needed more proven types of weapons,

such as battleships, tanks, artillery, jeeps, and rifles. They often argued that military planes should be designed mainly in attack and pursuit or fighter versions to help ground and naval forces fight their battles and not go off on their own missions far behind enemy lines.

The conservatives thought a war could be won only if enemy troops were defeated on the battlefield. They especially doubted the conviction Air Corps officers had about the ability of their bomber crews to find and destroy key military and industrial targets in pinpoint "surgical strikes." Here, the opposition was correct. The violent "carpet-bombing" raids flown by B-29s on Japanese cities near the war's end were not anticipated by the strategic-bombing planners. The "city-busting" technique was forced on them by the great difficulty and failure of "surgical strikes."

The opponents also realized that strategic bombing didn't need much help from the Army and Navy and worried that this new way to fight might lead to a new branch of the military, which would compete for prestige and for shares of the taxpayers' money. This sort of politicking and bureaucratic competition has always been an important part of the development of new weapons in America.

The new B-17 helped fight off strategic bombing's opponents. But as late as 1938, conservative military officers ordered cancellation of the B-17 and no new development of heavy bombers. Only in early 1939, just a few months after the Munich Conference and before the war in Europe began, did real support for the heavy bomber grow among people in the government such as Pres. Franklin D. Roosevelt, his aide Harry Hopkins, and Gen. George Marshall, the Army's new chief of staff. Until then, supporters of strategic bombing, such as Andrews and Arnold, had to play their cards carefully.

In late 1937, the bomber advocates "informally" asked some aircraft companies to consider how they might build a very long range bomber, one that was bigger and heavier, able to fly much further and faster than the Flying Fortress and carry a bigger bomb load, too. This was a tall order. The airplane would be a bold new design, powered by four 2,200-horsepower engines and 16-foot propellers. It would weigh nearly 125 tons. The B-17 weighed only about 30 tons. Unlike the B-17, the new plane would have "tricycle" landing gear. A wheel under the nose instead of under the tail made big airplanes safer in takeoff and landing and much easier to handle while taxiing around airbases.

The new bomber would be "supercharged" or "pressurized." This meant that the engine's intake of air would be compressed and heated and that the inside of the craft would be sealed off from the outside. The officers knew that the way to increase range and speed was to fly very high, well above the weather, at altitudes of more than 25,000 feet, where the air is much thinner and very cold. But they didn't want crewmen to have to wear heavy clothes during the long periods when they would be cruising through the stratosphere or oxygen gear to breathe and prevent "the bends," a dangerous ailment caused by too rapid a decrease in air pressure.

The Air Corps relied on the aircraft companies for new designs. The companies, however, weren't too excited about a new bomber. Company executives and engineers loved to think about pushing the technology as far as they could, but it cost a lot to design new airplanes. Engineers had to spend months at drawing boards and their salaries had to be paid. But in the 1930s, the law on how the military could pay for new weapons built by private businesses was quite a bit different from what it is today. Air Corps officers could sign fixed-price contracts only. Cost-plus contracts were not allowed by Congress and officers could not give designers money "up front." Payments could be made only when a new airplane had been built and actually flown. This meant the companies had to risk their own money to buy materials and tools and to pay engineers and the workers who built prototypes. It might be months, even years, before a new plane was finished and paid for. No one could accurately predict the final cost of designing a brand-new airplane, but "cost overruns" were not figured into the contracts. And there could be no guarantees for "follow-on" production orders.

These Air Corps contracts were very unattractive for aircraft companies, and it worsened as the technology became more complicated and expensive. Congressmen who oversaw the military budget every year insisted on closely controlling the military's business dealings. They worried that a system of advance payments or cost-plus contracts would ruin competition and cause the aircraft business to be controlled by just a few officers and large companies. During the 1930s, the new aircraft industry became a target for a group of congressmen and senators who feared what Americans later identified as the "military-industrial complex."

Aircraft companies therefore faced very risky business conditions. As one Boeing man put it: "There was no sound of coin in Uncle Sam's jeans; his pockets carried only marbles and chalk." Air Corps officers complained when the companies put little real effort into a very long range–bomber design, but weren't really surprised, either. General Robins realized in late 1937 that "there are very few airplane manufacturers, if any, who will start from scratch and invest at least the sum of $500,000 with the uncertain prospects of obtaining a contract." That was especially true in the case of the very long range bomber because the companies thought such an airplane would probably never be built—that the Air Corps was more or less just fishing. And, of course, the companies could only vaguely imagine what the great demand for new bombers would be in just a few years when World War II began.

Four companies responded to the Air Corps' request: the Boeing Company in Seattle, Douglas in Los Angeles, Consolidated in San Diego, and Sikorsky, a United Aircraft company in Hartford, Connecticut. Of the four, the Air Corps decided Douglas's design was best, but they complained of it being just a "rehash" of Douglas's latest airliner, the DC-4. Officers found this especially disappointing, since Douglas was the largest and most profitable aircraft company. If its executives wouldn't risk time and money on a new bomber, who would?

Consolidated, Sikorsky, and Boeing were all losing money. Boeing had an especially bad year in 1938. It lost a lot on the B-17 design because the Army wouldn't buy more and help the company cover its design costs. Boeing, with only 2,000 employees, could not afford to spend on a new bomber. If a federal government loan hadn't been arranged for Boeing in 1940, the company would have gone bankrupt. The Boeing name, now so prominent in global aerospace, might have become just an obscure reference in the aircraft industry's history.

The Boeing Company had difficult dealings with the federal government ever since the young William Edward Boeing started it in Seattle during World War I. He led the company until 1934, when he resigned and sold his stock because he resented how he and his company had been unfairly treated by congressmen and the newspapers. The new aircraft and airline companies shouldered much of the political frustration and anger Americans felt during the depths of the Great Depression, and popular suspicions that big business and stock market corruptions as well as personal favoritism defined the government's relations with warplane and air mail contractors like Boeing. The company kept the Boeing name, even though Boeing himself retired to a ranch near Seattle and was no longer involved. In 1956, he died at age 75, but lived long enough to witness the first flights of the Boeing B-52 bomber and the 707, forerunner of the great Boeing 700 series of airliners.

The political and financial disincentives for aircraft firms were not all that blocked a new very long range bomber. In November 1938, Americans elected many "isolationist" congressmen who did not want the United States involved in the trouble stirred up around the world by Nazi Germany, fascist Italy, and Imperial Japan. These congressmen wanted to focus military spending on "hemispheric defense"—the defense of the United States and the other countries of North and South America. This was not the kind of mission that believers in strategic bombing had in mind. They wanted to use airpower offensively and as a deterrent to countries that might start a war. But those who hoped for serious work to build a new bomber had to wait until the end of 1939, months after Germany invaded Poland and World War II began.

First steps toward the B-29 were taken in the summer of 1939 when General Arnold secretly ordered a group of officers and experts to discuss the Air Corps' problems and propose new plans. Its members included Charles Lindbergh, who worried about the size and abilities of the Luftwaffe, the Nazi air force. The board thought the Germans would probably conquer all of Europe and Britain as well, in which case American planes, even the B-17, wouldn't have bases close enough to Europe to do what they were suppose to do—attack the enemy's homeland.

The officers also worried about how the Nazis might be able to attack the Western Hemisphere from Africa and might even get air bases in South America. That meant that if U.S. bombers went to war, they would have to fight defensively. Industrial and civilian strategic targets might not be targets at all for the B-17s. They might have to attack forward military targets like airbases, invasionary fleets, and armored divisions under all kinds of conditions. The board members decided the United States needed a new, more flexible bomber. The requirements they had in mind pointed to a very large airplane that could meet what they thought were the new threats to the United States and still make long-range strategic attacks.

The key was a bigger fuselage, where bombs and fuel tanks could be loaded and interchanged depending on the mission. For strategic strikes, there would be enough fuel for the long flights and enough bombs to damage distant targets like factories. For shorter, defensive strikes, more bombs of different types could be dropped in devastating raids on frontline military targets.

Gen. George Marshall approved the board's proposals but the Air Corps' hands were tied until congressmen voted on whether taxpayer money could be spent on a new bomber. Finally, in November 1939, Congress agreed and by February 1940 the Air Corps was able to send aircraft companies "formal" design requests for a "superbomber" that could fly 400 MPH and carry a ton of bombs on a 5,000-mile mission.

Four companies on the West Coast responded—Boeing, Douglas, Consolidated, and Lockheed of Los Angeles. But again, each company risked whatever time and money they put into their proposals because the Air Corps wasn't allowed to pay up front for the designs. This meant that the companies put less energy into the expensive work than they might have. In addition, they were all quite busy expanding their plants and workforces to build more and more already proven aircraft for the Army, Navy, and Marines, and for foreign air forces, especially the British, French, Chinese, and Dutch.

Still, the four companies sent very long range–bomber proposals to the Air Corps in April 1940. The best came from Boeing and Consolidated in San Diego. The Air Corps gave both companies contracts to develop scale models for testing. But the very long range bomber remained an abstract and distant concept. Even though Congress gave nearly $3 billion for military aircraft in 1940 and allowed much more leeway in how the military could deal with aircraft companies, and even though France had fallen to the Nazis and it seemed England was next, the contracts signed with Boeing and Consolidated in June 1940 for their superbomber models were worth a mere $85,000 apiece.

Consolidated's design, the XB-32, was only an improvement on its B-24 Liberator, a four-engine bomber that first flew in late 1939 and compared with the B-17 in performance. Only the Boeing Company really took up the challenge and the risks of designing an entirely new airplane for the very long range role. Since 1938 Boeing had paid a handful of its best designers to think about a new superbomber. They gave their different ideas model numbers 316, 322, 333, 334, and 341.

Claire Egtvedt, Wellwood Beall, George Schairer, and Edward Wells led the Boeing design team, along with Boeing's chief test pilot, Eddie Allen. They played with different sizes and combinations of the advances already made in the B-17 and XB-15. They worked with variations of Boeing's large commercial transports, the Clipper flying boat and the Stratoliner, the latter having a pressurized cabin for high altitudes. Each design revolved around the new aircraft's most basic requirement—a large fuselage that could carry as many bombs and as much fuel as possible.

Model 341 held the most promise, so the Boeing team focused on it through most of 1939. It became the basis for Boeing's proposal in April 1940. The $85,000 mockup contract Boeing received in June 1940 was called Model 345. It was bigger and almost 12 tons heavier than the 341 because the Air Corps now demanded much more armor and other defensive equipment.

In Seattle, Boeing put more and more of its engineers to work on the mockup—as many as could be spared from the B-17 Flying Fortress project, which they were then gearing up for mass production. They worked as individuals or in ever-growing teams; Boeing's long-range work developed into the most complicated project ever attempted by engineers anywhere. By 1942, close to 3,500 Boeing engineers worked on the project, along with another 700 mechanics.

Some engineers worked on basic problems in research and development—aerodynamics, weight control, metals, structures, vibration, armament, and mechanical gear. They had none of the computers or other aids scientists and engineers now have. They used pencils, paper, slide rules, and wooden models. Others worked in groups and did detailed designs of the many systems and parts—the wings and control surfaces, the empennage or tail section, the landing gear, and the nacelles, which housed the engines and their mounts on the wings.

The project engineer, who oversaw the engineers, was responsible for coordinating the work and keeping it on line. He approved designs and blueprints and sent them to Boeing's shop, where workers made parts for the mockup. The project engineer was one of the few people with a sense of the overall project. Breaking down the project in this way sped it up and also helped keep it top secret.

As the Battle of Britain raged in September 1940, Boeing and the Air Corps signed a contract for two flying prototypes of Model 345, even though the mockup wasn't nearly finished. The Air Corps now called Model 345 the XB-29, short for "experimental bomber number 29," the twenty-ninth Army bomber project since the Martin B-1, which had been designed in 1918. An enormous airplane, the XB-29 tested the limits of the possible in large, heavy, and fast aircraft.

Boeing's engineers were very aggressive. If it worked as planned, the XB-29 would be the fastest and heaviest airplane ever built. Its fuselage measured 99 feet long, its wingspan 141 feet across, and its tail-tip almost 30 feet from the tarmac. The base weight was about 37 tons—27 of those in aluminum. But it would grow to nearly 58 tons, or 116,000 pounds, when engines, bombs, fuel, equipment, and crewmen were added.

Engineers expected the XB-29 to be able to cruise at 380 MPH at 25,000 feet. It would have a no-load range of 7,200 miles and the capacity for 20 tons of bombs. There would be a crew of ten: six men in the nose cabin—the pilot, copilot, navigator, bombardier, engineer, and forward gunner; three men—the radar man and two more gunners—in the waist behind the bomb bays; and one gunner alone in the tail to protect the rear. The pressurized nose and waist cabins would be connected by a crawl tunnel that ran along the aircraft above the bomb bay like a spinal cord.

The weight and power of the XB-29 would be twice that of the B-17, and its overall size half again as big. Yet the XB-29 had the same air resistance or air drag as the B-17 because of the new steps Boeing engineers took to streamline it. They gave the XB-29 many aerodynamic advances. They designed its nose in the shape of an eggshell so that the fuselage cut through the air smoothly and evenly. The fuselage was a straight cylinder that ran 40 feet until the tail structure began taking shape in a slowly tapered cone.

Often called the empennage, the tail carried the dorsal fin's high arch, the rudder, and the two stabilizers and elevators.

The XB-29's fuselage formed a smooth tube that cut down air drag outside and eased the structural load inside. It let the high air pressure that crewmen needed to act evenly against the inside of the structural frame. It also meant that big sections of the airplane had the same measurements and construction patterns. If the XB-29 went into production, workers could be hired who didn't have the skills of experienced aircraft workers. It was a bigger airplane, but could be built more easily, faster, and with less wasted material. Easy assembly of B-29s by inexperienced workers was a constant consideration for the designers.

The XB-29's landing gear was fully retractable, designed to disappear into the nacelles and nose after takeoff. An indication of how important that was and how well the XB-29 had been streamlined was that the aircraft's air drag doubled when the gear was down. Another important technique that reduced drag was rivet countersinking. The hundreds of thousands of small rivets that held the outer aluminum skin onto the aircraft's framework were kept flush with the skin's surface so that they had no profile against the passing air. And the sheets of aluminum that made up the skin were not overlapped but butt-joined for even greater smoothness.

The main factor in the XB-29's aerodynamics was its long, slender wing. Boeing designers called it "No. 117." They kept it narrow and thin so it would slice through the air more easily and more quickly when cruising. To get enough lift when the plane was moving slowly, especially during takeoff and landing, designers put air spoilers called Fowler Flaps into the rear of the wings. These flaps are common sights on big planes now but were new in 1940. Powered by electric motors, they reach out to catch the air and give the wing more lift when needed. The flaps then move back into the wing for cruising. A B-29 pilot could increase the wing area by 20 percent.

The wing was thin and narrow, but very strong. It had to be

because the wing load was 66 pounds per square foot, an amazing figure for the time and one that would grow as the B-29 steadily became heavier. The wing could support the aircraft, as well as the four engines and the fuel tanks built into it, because of the tight structural cohesion of the wing's frame and surfaces and the strength of the main wing beam. Known as the spar chord, this beam was made of heavy aluminum. It ran from just outside the two outboard engine nacelles and connected at the center inside the bomb bays. The spar chord formed the XB-29's structural heart.

The XB-29 weighed so much not just because it was so big but also because it carried many extras. The experiences of German and British aircrews in their battles during 1940 showed that the men needed bigger guns and would have to be protected from enemy antiaircraft shells and fighter plane machine-gun and cannon attacks. So the XB-29 was given plenty of heavy armor plate around the crew cabins. It also needed self-sealing fuel tanks that would prevent deadly fires and fuel losses when the big tanks inside the wings were penetrated by enemy shots. That meant coating the inside of the tanks with rubber that could close up holes and gashes if they weren't too big and the fuel didn't ignite.

The XB-29 also carried the weight of many advanced systems—radar, communications, navigation, heating, pressurization, supercharging, sound-proofing, and gunfire control. Since the XB-29 was pressurized, its gun turrets had to be sealed. Gunners couldn't fire through open doors or windows as they did on other bombers. The moving guns would be mounted outside the plane. Gunners fired at attackers by remote control, using complicated computers under development by Sperry and General Electric.

These systems needed many electric motors that increased overall weight, but they were only some of the 125 motors the XB-29 used to move its wing flaps, lift and lower its landing gear, open and close its bomb-bay doors, and so on. The motors' power came from a series of generators driven by the main engines. In case of engine failure or if the engines were off, a small gasoline engine supplied electric power. This engine, the auxiliary power unit, or APU, was called the "putt-putt." Many crewmen who came to rely on it said that the B-29 was really a five-engine plane.

In its September 1940 contract for two flyable prototypes, Boeing agreed to deliver the first XB-29 nineteen months later, in April 1942, and the second in June 1942. The contract was worth $3.6 million, although everyone knew this was only a ballpark figure, and it showed that the government had formally committed money to the project, which allowed Boeing to borrow money from banks, sign contracts with its suppliers, and get the work going.

Actually, Boeing would build the XB-29s on a cost plus–fixed fee basis. Once the planes were finished, the engineers' salaries, workers' wages, and the cost of materials and parts were added up by Boeing's accountants and checked by Air Corps officers. They figured out how much Boeing's equipment had depreciated during the work and tacked that on, too.

Boeing would be paid that amount, less whatever advances and progress payments the Air Corps had already made. It would also get a fee for managing the program—6 percent of the total cost. That fee would not increase if the costs turned out to be higher than originally thought. And Boeing would be given a percentage of all savings if the final costs were less than expected. Thus, Boeing had an incentive to keep costs under control.

The 6 percent fee was Boeing's profit since it was used to pay dividends to whoever owned Boeing Company stock and to make up for Boeing's expenses on its earlier designs. But since the company was not risking its own money in the contract, the 6 percent can be seen as a fee for services. Boeing executives, managers, and engineers were, more or less, employees of the government.

Much the same can be said for all the men and women involved with the Superfortress program during the war. The cost-plus system made a lot of Americans suspicious (and still does). It seemed contrary to old ideals of free enterprise and competition and made them think of "profiteering" and "feather-bedding" at the taxpayer's expense. Actually, hardly any of that happened. B-29 contracts were audited. Profit levels were solid, but not out of line. And there really was no other way to handle this kind of project. "It will be cost-plus or nothing," said the president of a major B-29 subcontractor, the Edward G. Budd Company of Philadelphia. No company could risk the old way—a fixed-price contract—on something as complicated and unpredictable as the B-29.

Congressmen finally recognized this. In the summer of 1940 the law was changed so that the Air Corps could deal with companies like Boeing in a more realistic way and compensate them for their work. High-technology military projects, like the B-29, required a much less adversarial relationship between government and industry than had been the case during the 1930s. A new partnership between the Army and Navy and aircraft companies emerged during the early years of World War II, a partnership based on mutual support, cooperation, high levels of spending, and rapid technological change that still define the relationship today.

In the case of the B-29 project, this relationship was very loosely based and suggests just how much of a leap of faith the program was for the Army Air Force officers. They worked with Boeing engineers and executives on thousands of details, but they were not heavily involved in design, overall planning, or, later on, in running the production program. The officers were there to think of and make the overall requirements for a "very long range bomber." And as the B-29 program evolved, officers and other government agents were always there to provide financing and to trouble-shoot big management problems when they arose. But basically federal officials took a hands-off approach and stayed in the background.

In October 1941, for instance, the general in charge of Air Corps dealings with the aircraft industry, Oliver P. Echols, wrote the following memo for his assistant on the B-29 project: "I do not know what setup you have for close follow up on this project, but I believe the time has come where we would be justified in having the Project Officer actually visit this project once a month and give you

a detailed report on progress being made." The B-29 was initiated by the Air Corps but it was very much a Boeing product.

General Arnold decided in October 1940 that the Air Corps would have twelve more XB-29s from Boeing. But he kept it a close secret until after the 1940 election. The United States was spending huge sums of money on the military but most Americans opposed U.S. involvement in the war. President Roosevelt reassured them in his election campaign speeches that the United States would fight only if attacked and that no American soldiers would be sent overseas. In this political environment, Air Corps officers had to keep their cards close to their chests because the B-29 was basically an offensive weapon. In December 1940, only one more was ordered.

Boeing engineers had developed a full-size wooden mock-up of

Wooden mockup of the XB-29, February 25, 1941. Courtesy of the Boeing Company (15783-B).

the XB-29 in November 1940. But well into the summer of 1941 it would still be just a paper proposal, an airplane based on faith. It existed in mockups and models, on about 8,000 blueprints, and in the minds and discussions of Boeing engineers and Air Corps officers.

The time it took to design the XB-29 worked against the project. Many planners and officers still opposed the long-range bomber, even in the Air Corps. Others insisted that the military threats of 1941 left no time and resources to spare for designing complicated new aircraft. The Army and Navy needed a lot of equipment right away. And Congress approved Lend-Lease, which made the U.S. defense industry a primary source for the British and Soviets who needed weapons immediately to fight the Germans. The XB-29 seemed a dangerous diversion of effort.

But General Arnold kept pushing. Others, like Henry Stimson, the secretary of war, and his assistant Robert A. Lovett, used their positions to prod the XB-29 along. Most important, President Roosevelt had decided in May 1941 that long-range bombers made up the center of U.S. strategy. He ordered the Air Corps to figure out how to get 500 bombers a month of all types. So solid was support for the long-range that contracts were given to Consolidated and Northrop to start designing the B-36 and the B-35, huge bombers even more ambitious than the B-29.

After FDR's call for 500 bombers a month, Boeing gave its best guess on costs and the amount in fees it needed to expand its XB-29 work. The next month, War Department officials approved a contract for fourteen YB-29s or "service test" B-29s. Planners

The XB-29 lifts off from Boeing Field on its first flight, September 21, 1942. Courtesy of the National Air and Space Museum, Smithsonian Institution (A-70114).

assumed that when these planes were ready, the project wouldn't be experimental anymore and that YB-29s would be used to test and train pilots and crew.

The YB-29 contract, worth nearly $20 million, was the base for all further B-29 orders from Boeing. It included Boeing's 6 percent fee but not the cost of engines, instruments, and other equipment, which the Air Corps supplied. It also did not include new factories and plant equipment. The federal government's Defense Plant Corporation and the Army Corps of Engineers paid for these. With all this support, Boeing promised to deliver YB-29s in January and February 1943, only a year and a half away.

During the fall of 1941, the XB-29 slowly took shape. But many still doubted the project. The new aircraft seemed too big for its wings. Then, in October 1941, the XB-29 received a solid vote of confidence when independent engineers from North American Aviation of Los Angeles went to Boeing–Seattle to look over the project "from a reasonably pessimistic viewpoint." One of them, James L. Atwood, said the XB-29's wing was more efficient than any he had seen. He thought it "very hard to find the right propeller," though, and rightly predicted that the XB-29 wouldn't fly in April 1942, as planned, but in September 1942. Still, Atwood wrote that Boeing was "doing a very fine job" and that it "looks like a good airplane from the production point of view."

Work continued on the XB-29 into 1942. As is common with experimental aircraft, its first flight had to be regularly rescheduled. In May 1942, workers had the XB-29 only one-third complete. But the aircraft gradually took shape and its components took a battery of tests to prove structural integrity. With the prototype almost ready, technicians jacked it up for weighing. They were amazed when the B-29's center of gravity came in within an inch of what engineers had predicted.

Finally, on September 21, 1942, the XB-29 was ready. Boeing's famous test pilot lifted the craft from Boeing Field and flew it for 75 minutes. "Eddie Allen reports that we have an excellent aircraft," read Boeing's telegraphed message to Washington, D.C. The next day, Donald Putt, a pilot in the new Army Air Forces, took up the XB-29 and said it was "unbelievable for such a large plane to be so easy on the controls." Flight tests went on. On December 2, 1942, the XB-29 reached 25,000 feet and on the thirtieth, the second XB-29 flew. Engineers needed many more months to iron out problems. But feelings ran high. One officer said, "You can fly it with one hand quite easily. . . . I wouldn't change the bet."

ARRANGING B-29 PRODUCTION

ven while the XB-29 was still experimental, and although it didn't fly until late September 1942, Boeing and government planners began putting much time and taxpayers' money into the B-29's mass production. By the end of 1942, about $3 billion was committed, the most spent on any single weapon project during the war, including the atomic bomb program. Some worried officers called the project the "$3 billion gamble" and wondered if the aircraft would succeed. Most involved, however, were confident. They thought the very long range bomber—also known as the very heavy bomber—was the weapon of the future. For them, the B-29 was a challenge calling for bold action. For the nation's security, it seemed worth $3 billion.

In early 1941, B-29 planners began a process now called "concurrency." In this process, workers, factories, and equipment are made ready for building a new product, even though it is still on the drawing boards and has not yet been proven to work. Today, concurrency is often criticized as too risky and likely to lead to expensive "cost overruns" or "white elephants." In spite of warnings, B-29 planners pushed ahead. They felt that most of the air-

frame's innovations had already been proven in craft such as the Stratoliner and Clipper, and that the XB-29's real gamble was the development of its equipment, especially its engines, props, and fire-control system.

In January 1941, the planners focused on the problems and costs of building seventy-five B-29s, with the idea of building hundreds more. At that point the B-29's cost was estimated at $1.5 million apiece. The airframe would be about $1 million, the engines $110,000, and the B-29's special equipment would make up the rest. The real cost of the B-29 was much higher, though, because many factories and expensive tools would be needed. These would either have to be taken from aircraft projects already at work or built brand-new.

The B-29's planners thought they would use the factories, machines, and workers already building Boeing's B-17. The Flying Fortress was well into production in 1941, but the program had problems. Once German fighters and antiaircraft guns illustrated the weaknesses in long-range bombers, changes were made to improve the B-17's performance. Its defects and limitations were gradually overcome by a combination of better equipment and crew

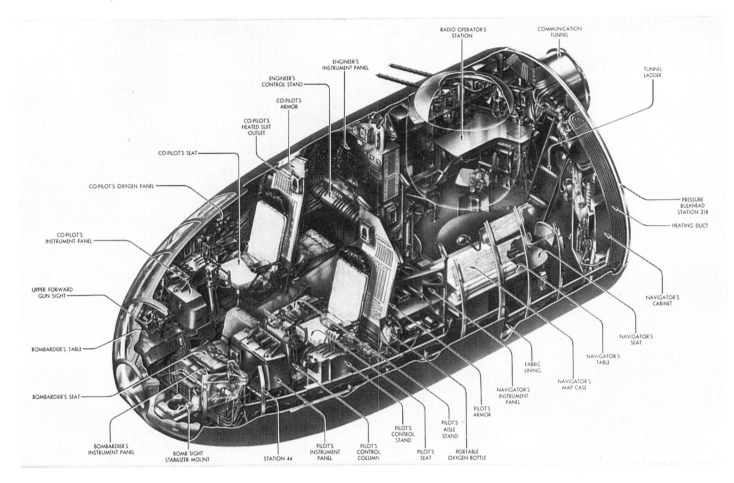

Cutaway of the forward pressurized compartment of the B-29 Superfortress. Courtesy of the Boeing Company (HS1000).

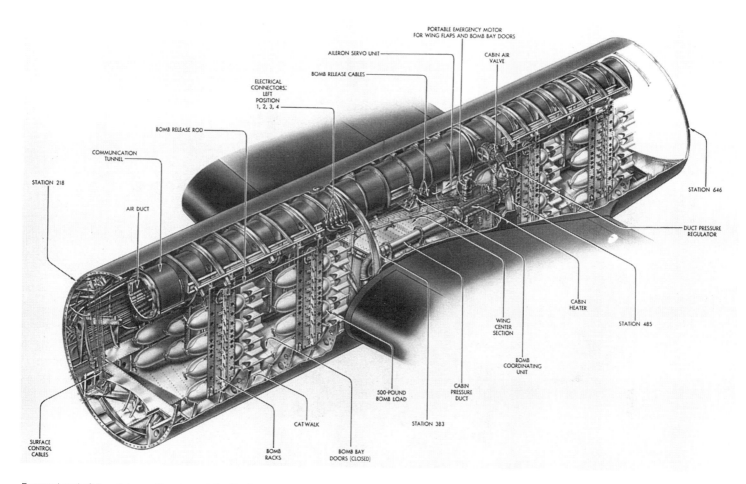

Forward and aft bomb bays. Courtesy of the Boeing Company (HS1000).

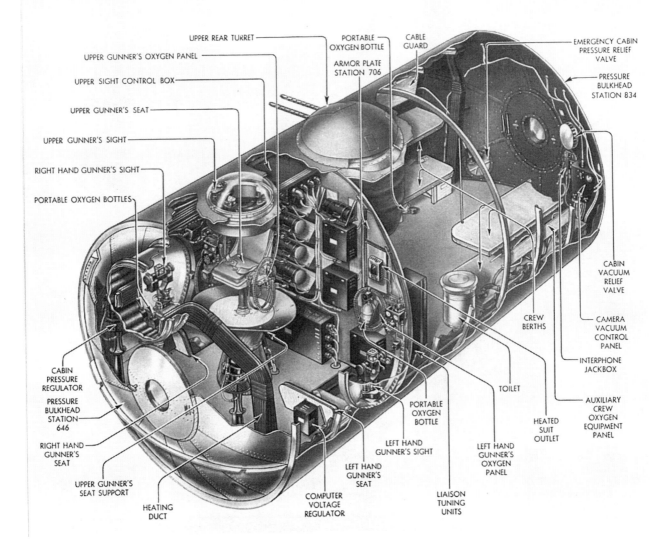

Aft pressurized compartment. Courtesy of the Boeing Company (HS1000).

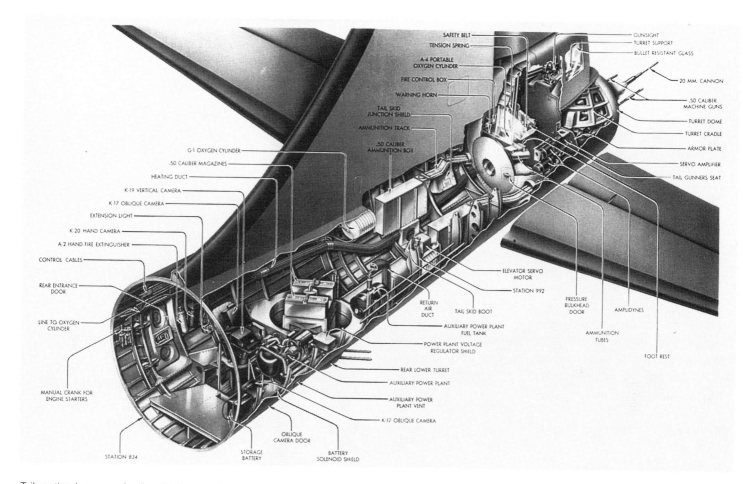

Tail section (unpressurized) and tail gunner's compartment. Courtesy of the Boeing Company (HS1000).

training, as well as the sheer number of B-17s turned out. The key to producing the vast amount of planes was a new manufacturing system arranged by aircraft industry executives and government officials, which included Boeing's new Plant 2 in Seattle, a giant new plant in Long Beach, California, operated by Douglas Aircraft, and another final assembly plant in Los Angeles managed by Vega, a Lockheed company. The group was known by its initials—the "B.D.V. consortium."

Incredibly, workers at those plants built nearly 12,700 B-17s by the end of the war. They were helped by workers at hundreds of other companies across the nation who fed parts and components to the three plants. Planners hoped that this well-oiled network could be converted for the B-29 sometime in 1942 when they thought B-17 production would be stopped. Meanwhile, they began setting up a separate network to get B-29 production going as soon as possible.

A new Boeing plant was being built in Wichita, Kansas; begun in October 1940, that plant had been in line to build B-17s, but in March 1941 it was tagged for the B-29. The government had given Boeing $13 million to build it and buy its equipment. The project was well underway when the Army Air Forces decided that the goal would be 25 B-29s a month. It would still be at least a year before production could begin at Wichita, but it would be at least that long before the B-29's design was finished. In April 1941, Boeing and the Air Corps agreed on a contract for 250 B-29s from Wichita, plus the equivalent of 25 B-29s in spare parts. A "letter of intent" worth $10 million sent to Boeing in May helped the company pay for equipment and other supplies while accountants and lawyers worked out contract details.

Preparations for building many B-29s continued through the summer of 1941, even though contract lawyers and accountants didn't finish Boeing's $215-million contract until early September. Planners faced many big challenges in such a large project as B-29 production. And the complications grew when President Roosevelt

called for 500 bombers per month. Under the Lend-Lease agreement between the United States and Great Britain, the Royal Air Force demanded as many bombers as it could get from American factories. With all these bombers ordered, the "B.D.V." system for B-17s could not be converted for B-29s. It would have to be expanded for more Forts.

This heavy demand also meant that Air Corps and company production experts had to keep focusing on the B-17 and on the B-24 Liberator. The B-24 was another heavy-bomber program using up huge shares of the nation's natural and human resources. The main B-24 plants were at Consolidated Aircraft in San Diego; Ford Motor at Willow Run near Detroit: and at Dallas–Fort Worth, where North American and Consolidated built Liberators in giant new branch plants.

The nation's engineers, production experts, and workers were kept very busy and in short supply, even to the point where Boeing did not have enough people to design and build the XB-29 on schedule. The problem was compounded by the Air Corps' secret plan to build more than 750 heavy bombers of all types every month beginning in December 1943.

Still, the new Boeing plant in Wichita for B-29s was well underway. Boeing agreed that Wichita would turn out twenty-five B-29s a month by May 1943, twenty-one months later. Another company also promised the Air Corps it would build B-29s. North American executives thought the government's new plant they were operating in Kansas City, Missouri, might be good for B-29s. They sent engineers to Seattle to look over the XB-29 in October. They agreed "to go ahead with 200 B-29s," assuming that "Boeing will make it work." The Army also called for more B-29 engines from Curtiss-Wright at Paterson, New Jersey.

Japan's attack on Pearl Harbor and Germany's declaration of war on the United States in December 1941 sped up planning. North American signed a deal to build 200 B-29s plus spare parts at Kansas City. The price was $187 million for the airframes alone. It included a 6 percent fee, plus a $1.3-million royalty to Boeing, a payment for the right to use the B-29 design. With the help of large advance payments up front from the government, North American executives felt very ambitious. They promised to start turning out B-29s in September 1943 and began placing orders for materials, production machinery, and other equipment.

During the next month, January 1942, Air Corps officers signed many contracts with companies for parts to be sent to the B-29 factories. General Motors accepted a $40-million deal to supply 6,600 of the B-29's huge propellers from its Frigidaire plant in Dayton, Ohio. GM's AC Spark Plug promised 1,000 automatic pilots. And General Electric signed on for B-29 fire-control sets from its plant in Schenectady, New York.

In the same month, a few weeks after Pearl Harbor, Air Corps officers made a massive extension to Boeing's contract. A total of 750 B-29s would come from Wichita at the rate of 50 per month beginning in June 1943. The new contract was worth a whopping $408 million. And Boeing was promised another $20 million to develop the government's factory in Wichita.

Meanwhile, Air Corps officers searched for a place to build another B-29 factory. In January 1942, they focused on the area around Atlanta, Georgia. They looked at a site that is now Hartsfield International Airport, but was then called Candler Field, after the man who invented Coca-Cola. But they decided that the town of Marietta, northwest of Atlanta, was better. The Bell Aircraft Company of Buffalo, New York, gave the Air Corps a commitment to provide experts to build 400 B-29s at the new "Government-Owned Aircraft Assembly Plant #6, Atlanta, Georgia."

General Motors also agreed to build 200 B-29s through its Fisher Body Division at a giant government-financed plant going up in Cleveland, Ohio. Air Corps officers and government officials were delighted that GM, the largest industrial company in the United States, became involved in B-29 final assembly.

Executives of the four companies—Boeing, Bell, North American, and Fisher—began meeting in early February 1942. With Air Corps officers they agreed to coordinate their work through a "B-29 Liaison Committee" that would vote on and maintain a "Controlling Schedule" for B-29 output. Major B-29 subcontractors were included—Chrysler, Goodyear, Hudson Motors, McDonnell of St. Louis, and Republic Aviation on Long Island, N.Y.

Officials of "civilian" government agencies, such as the War Production Board and the War Manpower Commission, or of trade unions, such as the International Association of Machinists and the United Auto Workers, were rarely involved in the liaison committee's work. Executives and managers of the member companies planned and coordinated B-29 production, with only occasional input from government people, including Air Corps officers.

Big military projects like the B-29 altered America's business system. But the hand of government planning and management never went much further than initiating project ideas, financing corporate America's efforts, allocating the scarcest materials, and handling temporary troubleshooting when labor or supply problems caused bottlenecks.

For most involved, it seemed important to preserve a sense of businessmen and corporations operating independently and voluntarily, free of government control. Army Gen. Kenneth B. Wolfe chaired the B-29 committee, but decisions took effect only when each company involved agreed. And the government, even though it had expanded greatly during the New Deal and World War II periods, didn't have enough of the right people with the right expertise to manage something as complicated as the B-29 project. Americans with professional administrative skills were mostly in private business and wanted to stay there. Most planners would have agreed with Col. Orval Cook, Production Division Chief at Wright Field in Dayton, Ohio, when he wrote that "the best results are secured . . . when there is a minimum of domination by the Army."

Boeing promised to supply the others with blueprint copies and the thousands of patterns, templates, gauges, jigs, and dies under design in Wichita. This equipment cut, stamped, and shaped the pieces of aluminum that made a B-29. They were key to "tooling up" the factories. Boeing also agreed that its accountants would show the others how to set up their contracts with the Army Air Forces and how to keep track of costs and inventories.

The goal was to get production going as soon as possible and to make sure the work in each factory was interchangeable. All B-29s had to be alike. Otherwise, repairing them and supplying them with spare parts would be too difficult. And the planners wanted "high production tooling." They wanted B-29 manufacturing to be quick and simple.

Workers in the different plants would concentrate on certain parts and ship them to each other. Fisher, for example, would supply the others with B-29 "subassemblies"—outer wing panels, tail surfaces, wing flaps, and engine nacelles. Each B-29 plant would have to build its own center wing sections. These were the B-29's structural heart, the 85-foot sections of wing built on the main spar. The center wing carried the engines, fuel tanks, bomb bays, landing gear, and the B-29's center of gravity. It was too big to ship from plant to plant.

"They're out to do a real job," said one government official about the B-29 committee. The B-29 was the biggest and most complicated thing Americans ever tried to build in large numbers. On those terms alone, the plans and efforts of the B-29 committee are impressive. What makes them truly striking is that the B-29 was still just an idea. Boeing didn't show that the XB-29 could fly until September 1942.

Hundreds of millions of taxpayer dollars were spent all across the country on the B-29 in 1941 and 1942. B-29 factories, machines, and tools, workers' wages and engineers' salaries were given high priority. The program made huge demands on the nation's supplies at a time when other military gear was urgently needed—ships, tanks, artillery, rifles, and fighter planes. President Roosevelt took personal interest in the B-29 and his assistant, Harry Hopkins, mon-

itored the B-29 program at the White House. After Pearl Harbor, expenses or effort on the B-29 were rarely spared, even though no one knew if it actually worked.

Through the spring of 1942, the B-29 committee built a national network of companies to feed raw material to the main plants, make production machinery for them, or supply parts on subcontract. The Boeing Company alone had 140 companies doing B-29 work on subcontract. Initially, the terms of these deals were left open because no one had a clear idea of what the B-29 would cost. The contracts had price figures, but they only represented a money commitment from the Army Air Forces that allowed companies to finance their "tool-up." Contracts would be "renegotiated" once actual costs were clearer.

In April 1942, accountants roughly guessed that once factories were built and equipped, the cost of the B-29 would be about $700,000 for workers' wages, the materials they used, and the plant's operating costs. A more accurate idea of total costs, however, included 30 percent extra for what was called "G.F.E."—government-furnished equipment. This included engines, guns, radios, radar, and other B-29 gear that the government contracted for and paid for separately.

Based on a price tag of $700,000 per plane, a $250-million contract was given to North American for 300 B-29s in April 1942. Bell agreed to build 400 B-29s for $342 million and to start turning them out of Marietta in September 1943. GM agreed to a $195-million deal for 200 B-29s and promised to use its plants and workers in Detroit, Memphis, and Muncie, Indiana, to build subassemblies for the factory in Cleveland. Of the full payment, 30 percent was made for these contracts in Air Corps "letters of intent" sent to companies months before the structure of contracts was agreed upon and signed.

In June 1942, the whole B-29 production plan was turned upside down. The members of the B-29 committee—under a lot of pressure—began arguing. They complained about delays in getting blueprints and data from Boeing. Boeing executives worried that leadership of the B-29 program might be lost to competing aircraft companies such as North American, Bell, or Douglas, whose executives and designers often resented having to build a competitor's model. They never trusted General Motors, which owned both Fisher and a large share of North American, the Los Angeles company just exploding in size. The pioneers of the American aircraft industry saw the big auto company as a threatening new competitor in the business. Meanwhile, GM people saw the opportunity and thought old aircraft companies should follow their lead because they had so much experience mass-producing cars, trucks, and buses while the aircraft industry had always been tiny. A worried General Echols said, "There appears to be considerable hard feeling."

Planners decided that North America's Kansas City plant would not be converted to B-29s after all, but would continue building its two-engine medium bomber, the B-25. Twelve of these Mitchells had just flown under Jimmy Doolittle's command from an aircraft carrier in a spectacular and much publicized raid on Tokyo. The Navy wanted more B-25s and wanted to deal. A Navy aircraft plant was going up in Renton, near Seattle. Boeing was supposed to build flying-boat patrol-bombers there, but the Navy offered the plant to the Army Air Forces for B-29s.

So North American was "eliminated from the B-29 picture." The Army Air Forces shifted B-29 commitments to Boeing–Renton, despite, in General Echols's words, the "complicated contractual involvement of cancelling the North American B-29 contracts and unravelling its subcontracting deals." The process kept hundreds of lawyers and accountants busy for months.

Boeing now set up to build 800 B-29s at Wichita and Renton. In July 1942, Boeing had B-29 contracts worth nearly $750 million, a figure that didn't include the costs of factory buildings and equipment, which the government paid for separately. Almost all the B-29s built were lost in battle or in accidents or junked for scrap when they became obsolete. But their runways, factory buildings, and much of their factory equipment are still in use. They represent the program's long-term "capital investment"—an important step among many others taken by the government during World War II in its ongoing role as a main financier of the nation's industrial, technological, and social development through the military business.

In August 1942, all assumed that Boeing, Bell, and Fisher would deliver 562 B-29s ready for combat by New Year's Day 1944. This was only the beginning. By the time the XB-29 first flew in late September 1942, 1,665 B-29s were ordered with their spare parts. Boeing promised 1,065 B-29s—765 from Wichita and 300 from Renton—while Bell would build 400, and GM–Fisher 200. Nearly $1.5 billion was committed to the B-29's airframes in 1942.

CHANGES AND PAINFUL DELAYS

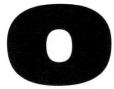Ordering B-29s was easy. Turning them out was something else indeed. Through 1942, 1943, and 1944, the B-29 program felt all the usual teething pains of a new aircraft and weapon system. For the Superfortress these normal problems became serious delays since it represented so much hope for victory and for the strategic bombing vision.

Planners and executives felt pressure to make good on the huge investment already made on the B-29. The project was pretty much a secret, but planners knew that one day they would have to account to taxpayers and congressmen for the huge sums of money spent. If the B-29 flopped, or wasn't ready until after the war, the names and reputations of companies, executives, and Army Air Force (AAF) officers would suffer badly.

To get the B-29 into combat quickly, planners drastically shortened the usual process of design, development, production, and deployment of a new warplane. They telescoped the process even more in April 1943 when General Arnold and General Marshall agreed to a "Plan for the Employment of the B-29 Airplane against Japan Proper" and approved an "acceleration program for the B-

29." At least 100 B-29s were supposed to be at forward bases by New Year's Day 1944, less than a year and a half after the XB-29 first flew.

But these early hopes for the B-29 were overwhelmed by problems and delays that seemed endless. It was hard enough setting up the factories and assembly lines and finding enough materials, subcontractors, and workers when the nation's economy was stretched near maximum to fill many war needs. These supply barriers only added to the basic problem: the B-29 and its subsystems were still experimental.

As the XB-29s made their flight tests, streams of changes to improve them and make them safer flowed through the production system—from the prime contractors to the "subs" and suppliers. "It is desired that the following modifications be made to the B-29," read just one high-level memo from AAF headquarters in Washington to the factories in early 1943. It listed complicated changes to armor and gun systems, bomb-bay doors, and "flame-damper" equipment around engine exhausts. Such changes were only part of an ongoing "change list" regularly sent to the manufacturers. These changes were essential for safety and military effectiveness and had to be made even though an impatient General Arnold ordered that the "design be frozen."

It often seemed that large numbers of B-29s would never get off the ground. Even a minor change could mean basic changes throughout such a complicated aircraft. A good measure of the problem is that for every hour spent by engineers on the XB-29, another ten were needed for changes in production B-29s. But AAF officers gave the program all the energy they could muster and squeezed every extra ounce of effort out of the manufacturers, engineers, and workers. The first production B-29 flew over Wichita in July 1943. Less than a year later, in June 1944, B-29s launched their first raids against enemy positions in Indochina.

By New Year's Day 1945, 750 B-29s were fighting overseas. To that point the Twentieth Air Force lost 142 B-29s to enemy action, breakdowns, or accidents. In March 1945, the 2,000th Superfortress was built. Well-supplied B-29 squadrons regularly attacked targets in Japan, pulverizing its cities with high explosives and firebombs.

Looking back, this time frame seems very short for a complex aircraft and weapon system like the B-29. For those involved with the program, however, it seemed like forever. Even though Boeing–Wichita managed to turn out seven flyaway B-29s as early as July 1943, the summer and fall of 1943 was a time of special crisis for the program. By January 1, 1944, only ninety-two B-29s had been built and only sixteen were combat-ready.

Design changes disrupted the program but shortages of workers and equipment at the major plants also caused delays. And in July, planners turned the final assembly program upside down again. They decided that GM–Fisher would not build the B-29 after all. The Glenn L. Martin Company of Baltimore, building two-engine B-26 Marauders at its new plant in Omaha, Nebraska, would take over Fisher's job. Final assembly would be left to the old names of the aircraft industry—Boeing, Bell, and Martin.

Fisher continued supplying B-29 nacelles but the company refo-

cused its Cleveland plant on the new P-75 fighter. This was unfortunate, not just because so many delays resulted from the transfer of contracts, subcontracts, and equipment for the B-29 from Cleveland to Omaha. The P-75 itself proved a failure and Fisher's efforts were wasted when the Army Air Forces canceled the project a year later.

Army officers signed an agreement with Martin–Nebraska in July 1943 allowing company executives to buy B-29 production gear. They redirected their main "subs"—Hudson, Chrysler, and Goodyear—from B-26 to B-29 work and promised they would be turning out twenty B-29s a month in July 1944. By October 1943, AAF officers committed $90 million to B-29s from Omaha, a figure that excludes the $25 million the government already put into the Omaha plant.

The shift to Omaha added to the program's delays—design changes and shortages of workers and materials. The impatient General Arnold decided to take drastic action. Calling it his "Must Program," he took the B-29 "out of channels." B-29 decisions could now be made without clearing so much military red tape. General Wolfe of the B-29 committee was now "authorized to deal directly with the manufacturers . . . in all matters that will assist in making the B-29 operationally and tactically suitable at the earliest possible date."

Arnold ordered that "any change, future or pending, be reviewed or eliminated unless it is necessary for the safety of the crew. . . . The airplane is good enough now and is to be left alone." He hoped sarcasm would help: "It is my desire that the airplane be produced in quantity so that it can be used in this war, not the next." He ordered production centralized at Boeing–Wichita. Engineering and production decisions came from there and every effort was made to increase output from the only plant turning out B-29s. The other plants would keep trying to meet their schedules, but they would first help Wichita find more tools, material, and parts.

The general also lifted official secrecy around the B-29, which speeded paperwork. Army public relations people used much fanfare to introduce the new bomber, trying to get everyone involved to work harder. Boeing executives and Air Force officers argued, however, about what the B-29's official name ought to be. Boeing wanted "Superfortress." But officers thought the name would draw too close a link in the public mind with the Boeing B-17 Flying Fortress and give Boeing too much credit for the B-29—even though the company deserved almost all the credit. The officers preferred B-29 "Annihilator." After a few months General Arnold decided to go with Superfortress.

General Arnold also threw his weight around Washington, D.C., clearing away political and bureaucratic obstacles to the B-29. He got General Marshall to give it "green light top priority." He fought off challenges from Navy people who thought "so much activity in connection with the drive to get the B-29 project rolling" was taking too much of the nation's war energy and resources. Arnold forced civilian agencies such as the War Labor Board and the War Manpower Commission to take up the special problems of B-29 workers, especially at Boeing's plant in Renton and at the Curtiss-Wright plant in Woodridge, New Jersey, where workers built B-29 engines.

But constant design changes and delays continued into 1944. Engines posed the biggest problem for the whole project but the B-29's computerized fire-control system was still a long way off. De-icing gear had to be put in the wing's leading edges. And the bomb-bay doors needed snap-opening mechanisms because slowly opening doors caused too much flight instability during the bomb run and showed enemy fighter pilots when the B-29 was most vulnerable.

Flight tests also showed the need for stronger observation blisters for the gunners, so that they couldn't get blown out of the pressurized craft. And the B-29's windows frosted over at high altitudes, making it hard for crewmen to see. A new type of glass and defrost equipment had to be designed and installed. The carburetors on the B-29's engines needed to be replaced by fuel-injection. And the pro-

pellers needed a better "feathering system" to allow the pilot to twist the prop blades when an engine failed so they wouldn't spin out of control and start fires.

At Bell–Marietta, company executives tried to cope with engineering changes that came forty-two times a week. They guessed they had lost a half-million worker hours by March 1944 but admitted they would never know for sure because "the records are far from being in shape." "It will take three months to regain the momentum in production," they warned, and said they feared what congressmen and taxpayers would say about all the delays and all the money spent in Georgia.

Design changes disrupted production lines but also delayed crew training on existing B-29s. New B-29s were flown not to

A B-29 wreck in 1944. Such mishaps were very dangerous, costly, frustrating, and all too frequent as engineers and workers struggled to iron out the B-29's many bugs. Courtesy of the National Air and Space Museum, Smithsonian Institution (5340-7A).

B-29s lined up on the tarmac in Wichita waiting for modifications. Courtesy of the Boeing Company (BW22148).

bases but to "modification centers" where workers made changes and fixed defects. Setting up these centers and paying people to do the work added much to the B-29's cost. Modification centers went up at Marietta and Omaha, but lining up aircraft to wait for modifications at the plants demoralized workers, so planners decided to do the work elsewhere as much as possible. Continental Airlines operated a major modification center at Stapleton Airport near Denver. And Bechtel-McCone-Parsons, the San Francisco management and construction firm, built and ran a sprawling new modification center at Birmingham, Alabama. At Birmingham alone, 5,200 workers struggled to make B-29s combat-ready.

Reworking B-29s was frustrating. The difficulty of quickly introducing changes into assembly caused bad feelings and finger-pointing among company executives and the military men, who were under heavy pressure from the White House to get the expensive Superfortress into the war. By the end of 1943, each B-29 needed about 25,000 worker hours for modification. Specially trained crews could work the B-29s only in groups of ten to twenty people at a time. Some B-29s were at the centers for more than sixty days, just sitting on tarmacs waiting their turns. By April 1944, 104 B-29s waited for modification. An Air Staff general understated things when he said the process was "extremely uneconomical."

The B-29's redesign problems had to be solved but none more quickly than engine overheating. It turned out that the B-29's engine, the mighty Radial-3350, was very difficult to keep cool. Many fatal crashes and "complete wrecks" during flight test and training missions over the new B-29 bases in Kansas were caused by engine fires. Even though these were among the B-29's most complicated parts, the engine nacelles and cowling had to be changed to allow more air to the engines' roaring eighteen cylinders.

"The B-29 program is in such a state of flux that it is very hard to keep a firm production schedule," wrote one discouraged officer in late 1943. Another was amazed at how far production and crew

training had gone while engineers were still "working the bugs out of the airplane." The automatic fire-control system, under test at Eglin Field in Florida, was so problematic that planners debated whether it should be given up. Some argued that the B-29 be built without pressurized cabins and with posts for crewmen to man the guns directly.

In February 1944, the commander of the new Twentieth Air Force complained that "not a single B-29 complete and ready for war has been delivered" to him at Smoky Hill Air Field in Salina, Kansas. Others complained that changes not only slowed B-29 output, they made B-29s "non-interchangeable," or different from one another, and thus much more complicated and expensive to maintain.

Some argued for canceling the program despite everything put into it. The situation called for another injection of General Arnold's energy. Helped by Robert Lovett, assistant secretary of war for air, Arnold defended the program at the White House and in the War Department. He ordered greater effort from everyone and re-arranged command, including the appointment of Gen. William Knudsen, formerly president of General Motors, as coordinator of the B-29 program.

Arnold and Lovett were not deterred by the fact that the deadly experiences of heavy bomber crews in Europe had led their planners to predict a brutal career for the B-29. They pegged B-29 "attrition" rates at 63 percent per operational tour. The Air Staff expected that two of three B-29s would be lost in combat and their crews killed or captured every thirty missions. Nor were top officials deterred by their new knowledge of the impracticality of "surgical strikes." This strategic-bombing ideal would have to give way to area bombing of enemy urban centers.

Everyone's efforts on the B-29 began paying off in a slow but steady stream of progress. In April 1944, Boeing–Wichita delivered thirty-six B-29s, boosting its total to 267. In the same month, Renton built three B-29s for a total of eleven; and Bell–Marietta, twelve for thirty-one. But problems didn't disappear. Workers injected many complicated changes into the assembly process, but the B-29s still needed some 61,000 worker hours at the modification centers. That meant some 1,500 people working a forty-hour week for each plane and about half the effort that went into building the aircraft from scratch.

In May 1944, Bell had twenty B-29s in modification at Marietta. Another nineteen were added in that month but only twelve released. At Bechtel–Birmingham, thirty B-29s just sat on the tarmac. One officer nervously thought about the crusty General Arnold. "If the old man would see that . . . Christ, he's just going to go through the roof."

Most everyone involved with B-29 planning "expressed keen disappointment with Bell" and also complained about Renton. These plants started later, but proved less able to learn from Wichita or get design changes into original assembly. Planners gave up on Bell and ordered production managers there to stop trying because they were not "modification-minded." They got "open instructions to build all B-29s possible," "stripped ships as they stood," and sent them on to be modified at Birmingham.

Modification workers managed to reduce the time B-29s spent at the centers to about nine weeks, even though changes continued to come in as more was learned from the Far East about how the B-29 actually performed in battle. In August 1944, officers ordered an emergency program to reduce the B-29's weight. "The present B-29 as it leaves the modification center is definitely too heavy," wrote a planner. Too many extra installations made takeoffs too risky. The Superfortress was getting too hard to lift off the runways. Air speed and range had fallen while wing loading grew to 77 pounds. Many extras not absolutely critical to aircraft performance were deleted, including the B-29's coat of camouflage paint. The weight-loss program shaved nearly 10 tons but at the cost of still more modification and delays.

Bottlenecks continued through most of 1944. One general explained that delays were "due to the fact that the B-29 is not entirely out of the woods from an engineering standpoint." Still, planners, engineers, and workers made steady progress. Their successes were partly due to the gradual rearrangement of resources and production schedules among the four main plants, the subcontractors, and the modification centers. But if not for the people of Wichita, and their special ability to fit changes quickly into assembly and get B-29s to the air bases, the program would have come to a standstill. Boeing–Wichita is the real success story of B-29 production.

WHY WICHITA?

**W**hy did planners decide that the main site for B-29 production would be on the plains of south-central Kansas? Why build a Superfortress nest at Wichita, a small city of 120,000 people on the Arkansas River and the old Chisholm Trail?

A basic consideration was the possibility of air and naval attacks against the continental United States. Government planners worried about invasions. It seemed essential to build key defense plants as far away as possible from the nation's borders and coastlines. These fears seem exaggerated now. But then, they were very real for many Americans.

Another basic consideration was that during these years defense work had swamped the nation's major industrial centers. Seattle, Los Angeles, and Baltimore not only became homes for huge aircraft plants, they were major shipbuilding cities, too. Employers found it harder and harder to find people who needed a job and could do the work.

Setting up new plants in America's rural heartland helped relieve this pressure. The economies of the farm belt and Southern states had not recovered from the Great Depression. It made sense to take defense work to the people in these areas, rather than have them move to the big cities and worsen the overcrowding.

And planners thought rural Americans would make solid aircraft workers. Most had good work habits and direct experience with mechanical equipment—trucks, cars, and farm equipment. They wouldn't be too intimidated by the machines and technical systems of a giant aircraft plant. Planners also thought about all the money that could be saved because of the lower wage levels in these areas. Since the cost of living was also lower, there would be no upward pressure on wages as in the big cities where workers were scarce and labor unions stronger.

On a darker note, planners found America's heartland attractive for expansion because so many of the people were so-called native-born Americans. Planners were prejudiced against immigrants and "hyphenated Americans" whom they thought more likely to start militant unions, or be Socialists, Communists, or Nazis who might be disruptive and even try to sabotage defense plants.

Wichita fit the bill perfectly. It was practically the geographic dead-center of the United States, nearly the same distance from all seacoasts and borders. And there were plenty of strong "native-born" young people who wanted jobs. More important, Wichita had a pool of solid experience in aircraft building that few other towns and cities had. It was home to some small but famous aircraft companies—Beech, Cessna, and Stearman—which with other companies had been turning out over the past twenty years small Army and Navy trainers and "puddle-jumpers" for the personal plane market.

Wichita had an airplane industry because men like Walter Beech, Clyde Cessna, and Lloyd Stearman lived there. "Pilots like the big fields," according to one newspaper. "50 per cent of Kansas farms have natural landing fields. . . . Kansas is a continuous landing field." There were good winds and "fogs are rare in Wichita . . . it's clear 90 per cent of the time." Much was made of how the people of the Kansas Plains had a natural sense of the winds and a strong incentive to use airplanes to overcome distances that seemed endless. And men who had succeeded in the local oil and meatpacking businesses willingly invested in these little companies.

Wichita aircraft companies and workers thrived during the 1920s, turning out one in four of the nation's commercial planes. But business turned bad during the Depression. Orders picked up in the late 1930s, mainly because of Army orders for the PT-17 Kaydet trainer built by Stearman, a company that Boeing bought up in the late 1920s. In January 1940, about 1,500 people worked on airplanes in Wichita, mostly at Stearman, which also built B-17 parts sent to Seattle. The company had about forty engineers.

This seems like a small, almost insignificant number of workers, especially when compared with the tens of thousands in the Douglas and Lockheed plants in Los Angeles, the Curtiss and Bell plants in Buffalo, or the 40,000 people who planners expected to put to work on Wichita B-29s. But this tiny group was crucial in making the Wichita plant the most successful builder of B-29s.

Most of these workers were highly skilled engineers and craftspeople—carpenters, machinists, sheetmetal workers, and electricians—who understood all aspects of building airplanes. They became the supervisors and foremen who set up the B-29 plant and showed new workers how to do their jobs. They gave the push and momentum to the great B-29 program at Wichita and secured the little city's future as one of the most important aerospace centers of the world.

Other factors help explain "why Wichita?" such as the city's Chamber of Commerce, which sent men to Washington, D.C., to lobby in Congress and at the War Department to make sure Wichita got its share of defense contracts. They bragged about Wichita's "highly competent laborers, most of whom are native[-born] American." And Wichita's city council financed early development of what became the B-29 plant site. It paid for a new runway at the municipal airport next to the Stearman plant on South Oliver Street and for new sewers and roads.

Wichita set up private and public schools to teach aircraft factory skills. These schools also could be expanded quickly. For the Boeing Company, primarily responsible for B-29 production, Wichita was a familiar place. The company had an organizational head start there and competent executives who could be relied on, such as Stearman's president J. E. Schaefer and chief engineer Harold Zipp.

Still, the main reason for the location of a giant B-29 plant in Wichita were the skilled aircraft workers already there and the clear potential for rapid expansion. In mid-1940, these people kept aircraft production 35 percent ahead of schedule, which deeply impressed Air Corps officers. In April 1939, Air Corps general George Brett secretly reported to the White House on his tour of the nation's aircraft plants that Wichita "is in excellent shape."

Local newspapers reported how the people of Wichita hated the Germans and Japanese for their aggressions and thought Adolf Hitler and the Nazis a bunch of "monsters" and "snakes." Most were delighted and excited, however, by the boom in their economy caused by World War II. Rumors swirled about how much the local aircraft business would be expanded. No one yet imagined what the B-29 would bring, which was secret and wasn't slated for Wichita until the spring of 1941. And the United States wouldn't be at war until December 1941. Still, in 1940, local news headlines read: "Good News," "Progress," "Prosperity Wave Is Evident . . . Real Estate Boom." City leaders "radiated optimism over the general economic outlook. . . . Prospect is rosy in the extreme."

A "$62 million tornado" hit Wichita in the summer of 1940. Orders for trainers poured in. Storekeepers looked forward to their best Christmas sales ever. "War Defense money came to Wichita in a blast," wrote one newsman. In September 1940, the people of Wichita learned that the U.S. Defense Plant Corporation, the government agency that financed the expansion of military industries, was planning Plant 2, a giant new factory to go up south of the Stearman works and to be operated by Boeing for B-17 production. Plans for a new Air National Guard base were also in the works at Municipal Airport, adjacent to the Boeing site.

Local people admired the new "forests of steel," the frames of new factories and hangars sprouting at Stearman, Beech, Cessna, and the Air Corps sites. In October 1940, workers broke ground for the huge new Plant 2, which is still a major Boeing facility in Wichita. The Austin Company of Cleveland handled design and construction on a cost plus–fixed fee contract. Sparing no expense, it used the very best construction materials and techniques and the latest equipment for air conditioning, heating, fluorescent lighting, plumbing, sprinklers, crane, and conveyor systems.

When the project was complete, total floor area of the Boeing–Wichita works measured 2.8 million square feet, including offices, warehouses, hangars, guardhouses, and the "camouflage building." The buildings enclosed 86 million cubic feet. With the new runway and taxiing areas, the whole project used 185 acres of land and cost taxpayers $26 million. Plant 2's main assembly floor covered an area of more than 1.7 million square feet. The two main assembly bays each measured 750 feet long, the biggest and highest unobstructed covered areas anywhere in the United States, and probably in the whole world.

The thirty-two steel trusses that carried the roof over the main bays stretched 300 feet. At 120 tons, they were the heaviest trusses ever used in a factory. They weighed almost as much as a fully loaded B-29. Their bottom chords were 45 feet above the concrete floor, which left plenty of room for the B-29's 30-foot tail. The trusses above the giant sliding doors along the plant's north side were even bigger, weighing 140 tons.

Since Wichita was so far away from possible air attacks, a "sawtooth" roof could be used instead of the more expensive flat-roofed "blackout" design used in new aircraft plants in coastal cities. This meant that windows, or "clerestories," could be built into the roof, which provided plenty of natural light and ventilation for the big area below. From a distance, the "sawtooth" roof gave it an older look, but Plant 2 was one of the most advanced factories in the world.

Soon, 2,000 people worked on the new plant—truck and tractor drivers, carpenters, concrete workers, steel riggers, block layers, electricians, roofers, and so on through the trades. By June 1941, the building was nearly finished. Some 3,000 people were already building B-17 parts to go by railroad to Seattle and Los Angeles. Or they set up machinery, stamping and cutting tools, and assembly jigs for the B-29, equipment that cost more than $40 million.

Even though the decision to go with the B-29 at Wichita had been made back in February, few people had any idea about the secret bomber. Only in August 1941, when 14,000 people worked at the plant, did a local newspaper vaguely report that "a new type of flying fortress will be built." The first big contract was signed in September—250 Wichita B-29s for $215 million. But the B-29 remained an "official" secret—a poorly kept one—until fall 1943.

The employment explosion continued at Boeing–Stearman and the other Wichita aircraft plants. The city was also a major supplier of other military goods, like tents and camp equipment by the Coleman Company. Among all U.S. cities up to 1944, Wichita had

Defense Plant Corporation photo of the Wichita works and runways. Plant 2, the warehouses, administration building, flight hangars, and overhead ramps are in the foreground. The old Boeing–Stearman Plant 1 is at left center. The Wichita Municipal Airport is at the right and beyond it the base that became McConnell Air Force Base. It was named after two local crewmen killed in action in the South Pacific and is now home to a wing of B-1 bombers. To the north is Planeview, built on Wichita's southern outskirts by the Federal Housing Authority. Courtesy of the National Archives.

Jigs for assembling the B-29's center wing section at Wichita. A big problem for mass production was including design changes to the wing that made it stronger and able to support the B-29, which continually got heavier and heavier as the Army Air Forces insisted that more and more extras be added on. Courtesy of the Boeing Company (BW4278).

Kansas women inside the B-29's pressurized crawl tunnel over a B-29 bomb-bay section. The crawl tunnel provided access for crewmen moving between the B-29s forward and waist cabins safe from the cold and low pressure at high altitude. Courtesy of the Boeing Company (BW21148).

the largest percentage of growth in the number of new factory workers. Their numbers grew by a factor of 8.5 over 1939. People soon began feeling the strains of labor shortages, overcrowding, and congestion.

But while such problems often caused crisis situations in other "defense cities," at Wichita they stayed manageable, due in part to the large pool of unemployed in Kansas and its neighbor states who were willing to work, and the foresight of federal, state, and local officials, and Boeing executives, who made many provisions for easing workers' lives. As early as the spring of 1941, for example,

construction began on 450 houses just north of the plant, a new community called Planeview. Some 6,000 homes went up for aircraft workers, 4,500 of them built by the Federal Housing Authority, the rest by private developers.

Officials also oversaw new schools, day-care centers, movie theaters, shopping malls, highways, and parking lots. They set up a service of fifty-four buses to move people quickly from points in Wichita and from towns within a 70-mile radius. When workers arrived at Plant 2, they passed through security, walked down four main stairways, put their things in lockers, punched the clock, and found their way through the vast basement where parts were stored. Stairways took them up to the plant floor and their workstations. Getting to and from work was unpaid time for workers and they appreciated how it was minimized at Plant 2.

"Rolling cafeterias," another much-appreciated provision for the workers, moved around Plant 2's departments, dishing out hot food, soup, coffee, tea, and pie for only $.28. "This beats any meal I ever had anywhere," beamed one young man. "That's the biggest meal I ever bought in Wichita," said a forklift driver. For one foreman, the "Great Boeing Kitchen" meant "my men don't gripe so much about their wives as they used to." So rich and deep was the local and regional labor supply that Boeing–Wichita (the Stearman name was dropped in 1941) could hire more than 1,000 people in December 1941 alone, and didn't need to hire many women for production jobs until the spring of 1942. "There has been no tendency to hire women . . . only as the factories find it impossible to get men for the jobs."

Until it became obvious just what women could do and how basic their labors were for the program's success, most people were uncomfortable with the idea of women working in factories. Local newspapers tried to break down the prejudices by running stories on how some housewives had gotten "permission" from their husbands to go to work and suggesting how other husbands should do likewise.

I'm Proud... *my husband wants me to do my part*

SEE YOUR U. S. EMPLOYMENT SERVICE
WAR MANPOWER COMMISSION

Images like these appeared as posters and advertisements in Wichita to try to help men and women overcome traditional attitudes on a woman's proper role. Courtesy of the National Archives.

"Her business is to be efficient, intelligent and to add her bit to as many planes as possible," ran a story about unmarried women at work. "She's a woman out to get her man, but right now the 'man' is the enemy." By Christmas 1942, women made up 35 percent of some 22,000 Boeing workers in Wichita. Planners expected that "60 per cent of the plane-makers at the big plant will soon be members of what used to be the weaker sex. . . . Manpower is fast becoming womanpower." The actual proportion of women workers never went beyond 40 percent.

Mixing men and women in production work caused problems, some surprising and others not so surprising. For example, the men lost time because they "glance at the women." Managers "segregated" women from men as much as possible, not just because of "roaming eyes"—male and female—but because supervisors discovered that work rhythms were "unbalanced" between the sexes. "Women tend to work faster early in the day while men work faster in the afternoon." Such observations were usually valid, but they also tended to reinforce biases and encourage the segregation of men's work from less-skilled and poorer-paying jobs held by women. Few women rose to management, supervisory, or skilled positions, but the key production jobs they and the men did accorded with the relatively new principle of "equal pay for equal work."

The women weren't always required to wear them, but managers designed special work clothes for the "defensettes," which they hoped would make them less distracting for the men. Safety concerns were just as important. One-piece "togs," fitting snugly from neck to shoes, meant no loose clothing that might catch in machinery or on scaffolds. A turban also prevented accidents that might be caused by loose, long hair. It also "assures a fresh, bright looking head of hair at the end of the day."

It seems a long time between the first big order in September 1941 to the first flight of a Wichita B-29 on June 29, 1943. Actually, it is surprising it wasn't much longer. The XB-29 didn't fly until September 1942 and remained an experimental project through

Working on a bomb-bay door at Wichita. Courtesy of the Boeing Company (X974).

A Superfortress rolls out of Wichita-Plant 2 during a rainy night shift in 1944. Courtesy of the Boeing Company (BW21232A).

much of its test-flight stage well into 1943. Constant design changes, national shortages of machine tools, aluminum, and steel, and the great complications of setting up production equipment on the scale planned for Wichita all had to be overcome before production B-29s could be built.

Boeing workers made Wichita the most reliable and efficient source of B-29s. Productivity steadily increased: on average, 157,000 worker hours were needed for each of the first 100 B-29s; 78,000 for the second 100; and 57,000 for the third. By late 1944, the figure had fallen to a steady 30,000 hours. By the end of 1944, workers turned out B-29s at the rate of 100 per month or nearly 4 per day. Wichita Superfortress number 1,000 rolled out of Plant 2 on February 14, 1945. In all, 1,769 Wichita B-29s were built—about 44 percent of the national total. And Boeing workers fit the endless stream of modifications into the production process much more quickly than elsewhere. By March 1945, B-29s rolling out the doors of Plant 2 were practically combat-ready.

Boeing–Wichita workers also built 10,346 tiny Kaydets, or 44 percent of all primary trainers needed by the Army and Navy after Pearl Harbor, as well as many troop-carrying gliders used in the D-day operations in France. Moreover, they kept a flow of spare parts going so that aircraft could be maintained and repaired in the field. Boeing–Wichita received five Army and Navy E Awards at a time when only 4 percent of defense plants in the United States received even one of these coveted awards for production excellence.

Plant 2 was the model for the other B-29 assembly plants—Marietta, Renton, and Omaha. Its productivity was held up as the standard against which it was hoped the others would perform. When the others struggled with bottlenecks and delays that became especially severe in the fall of 1943, planners turned to Wichita for increased output and a source of confidence that there efforts were going to pay off. In November 1944, planners once again "accelerated" output at Wichita "in order to fully benefit from production efficiency at the Boeing–Wichita B-29 plant."

Unlike at the other plants, and just about everywhere else in the nation's aircraft industry, the 26,000 workers at Boeing, and the 10,000 at the other Wichita aircraft factories, accepted a long 10-hour shift, seven days a week, with every other weekend off. This schedule drew all the energy workers could muster. The first shift started at 6:00 in the morning and ended at 4:45 P.M. Workers had 45 minutes for lunch. The second shift started at 4:45 in the afternoon and ended at 3:30 A.M. Workers' lives were grueling but many inefficiencies were reduced, such as a third-shift change. Once, when the Army Air Forces desperately tried to get B-29s into combat on schedule in 1944, Boeing–Wichita workers put in 21 consecutive 10-hour days!

Wichita aircraft workers, the large majority of whom came from the area or from Oklahoma, Arkansas, eastern Colorado, and western Missouri, were dedicated, able, and conservative. They showed little of the interest in unions or desire for worker participation in company decisions—especially on how work was organized—that workers in other areas and industries did. They weren't consulted on the 10-hour day and the company arbitrarily imposed its system of pay scales and job classifications.

They received time-and-a-half for every hour beyond 40 per week. But their base wages were much less than in other defense industries and the government always stalled efforts to "stabilize" or equalize wartime wages nationally, trying to suppress price inflation. The situation for Boeing workers became really galling when the government approved small wage increases for aircraft workers down the road at Beech and Cessna, but not for those at Plant 2. Meanwhile, inflation in living costs in Wichita increased by 25 percent in the years 1940–43.

Yet there's not much evidence of worker complaints or serious interest in unions or strikes. The absentee rate was very low. Few workers quit for better paying jobs or to go back to the farm. Boeing–Wichita B-29 production was possible because of this steady, solid force of workers. They were proud of their work and

An inspector checks B-29 nacelles before the engines, superchargers, cowling, prop assemblies, and landing gear are attached. This part of the B-29 posed some of the most complicated manufacturing challenges. When production began at Wichita, it took about 500 mechanics two shifts to get four nacelles and engines ready. By 1945, as the "learning curve" rose, 160 mechanics could get 16 nacelles ready in the same time. Courtesy of the Boeing Company (X143).

its contribution to the war effort. The company's worker newspaper regularly used such racial slurs and disturbing expressions as "Jap-blasting," "incineration," and "de-housing" to describe what the B-29s were doing to Japanese cities. The idea was to keep up workers' morale by playing on their bitter feelings for the Japanese.

James Schaefer, Boeing vice-president in charge at Wichita, accurately summed up the situation: "Everyone appreciates the fact that our hours are long, that this Kansas summer weather is hot, and that building B-29s is a tedious, hard job. The reputation earned by the men and women of Boeing–Wichita is and will continue to be one of high standing."

Only in late 1944, when it seemed the war's end was near and that people ought to get a head start landing "peacetime" jobs, did Boeing have trouble keeping workers. But by then, workers had become so productive and had so much experience building the Superfortress that more B-29s could be built with fewer workers. In 1945, the plant operated at full capacity in a kind of cruise-control mode, steadily turning out about 100 B-29s a month. When B-29 work was suddenly canceled at Wichita after the Japanese surrendered, a total of 1,634 had been built, the largest total of the four B-29 plants.

Boeing–Wichita Plant 2 was the first factory pegged for the B-29 and the first to turn out the big bomber. Its manufacturing system served as the model for the three other B-29 plants—Marietta, Omaha, and Renton—although each had their own unique features, depending on local conditions. Plant 2 was itself based on the system used by Boeing, Douglas, and Vega-Lockheed to mass-produce B-17s. Led by Oliver West, the talented chief of production engineering at Boeing, executives from these companies came up with the "multi-line assembly system" in 1940–41.

Wichita was arranged accordingly. The multiline system was a very innovative approach to the complex job of mass-producing a big, intricate object like a bomber. Production planners took many tips from the auto industry's assembly lines but applied them in ways that made more sense for aircraft. The most obvious difference between a factory for bombers and a plant for cars, trucks, or tanks was that the bomber plant was a big square or near-square rectangle while the auto plant was usually a long rectangle. Planners replaced the long assembly lines of the auto plant with short ones for bombers.

It was not practical to assemble bombers like cars and trucks on long, moving assembly lines that went past workers who attached more and more parts to the chassis until the final product drove out the factory door because bombers were too big and complicated. They didn't have the stable chassis of a car or truck. To build a bomber around its "chassis"—the main wing spar—would have been much too awkward. Aircraft workers couldn't stand on the floor and reach into whatever part of the bomber they were working on as it passed by, the way autoworkers could. To build a B-17 or a B-29 step by step on a moving line would have meant a maze of ladders and scaffolds that moved down the line with the bombers as they took shape.

Workers would need an array of hoists and pulleys because most parts were too bulky and heavy for people to handle. And workers needed more time at their jobs because aircraft work required a finer, more careful touch than cars. Aluminum was much less forgiving of mistakes and carelessness than the iron and steel used in cars. And aircraft assembly had fitting "tolerances" at much higher levels than cars. Aircraft parts had to fit much more exactly.

The answer for the bombers was the multiline system. Instead of one long final assembly line, workers set up six groups of lines, arranged around two or three short final assembly lines along the plant's main doors. Workers separately assembled the bombers' main pieces in "precompleted" form with all equipment installed. The idea was to keep B-29 parts as small as possible until final assembly and rollout from the plant. Six main groups of lines were set up for the nose, or forward fuselage section; the center section

9-28-43   FRONT PRESSURE CABIN ASSEMBLIES   BW-21.076

B-29 nose sections lined up at Wichita for installation of flight-deck equipment. Courtesy of the Boeing Company (BW21076).

A staged photo of a disassembled B-29 in Wichita to illustrate the main components of its final assembly: nose; bomb bays; tail; main wing section; outboard wing sections; and engine nacelles. Courtesy of the Boeing Company (BW24040).

All installations were made on the B-29's sections before final assembly. Courtesy of the Boeing Company (X975).

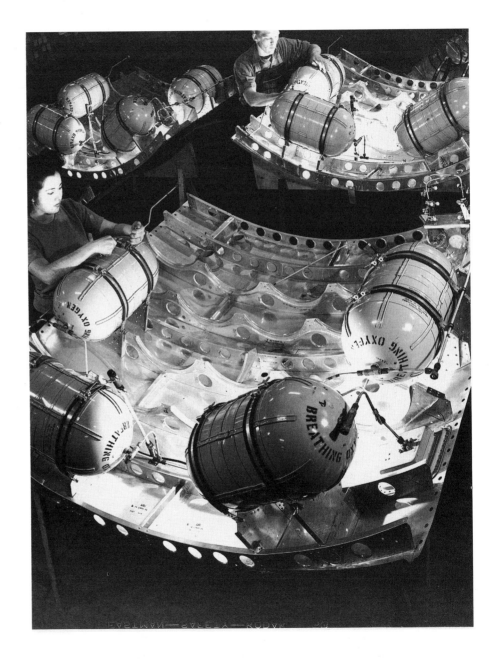

of the fuselage, or bomb bays; the tail section, or empennage; the center wing section built on the main wing spar; the engine nacelle arrangement; and the outboard wing and leading edge assemblies.

Each group of assembly lines gathered parts from shops around them on pushcarts, forklifts, or conveyor belts. In these shops, usually toward the factory's outside walls, workers operated the machinery that cut, pressed, bent, and welded raw aluminum and steel into parts. Or they did subassembly work on parts and equipment, like landing gear, turrets, and control surfaces for the wings and tail.

When workers completed one of the six main sections, giant cranes hoisted it up and brought it to the huge final assembly bays. The most dramatic part of B-29 production was the aircraft quickly taking final shape. At Wichita, it was quite a show: four rows of B-29s moving through five stations as workers joined up the six basic pieces. The job was mainly a matter of bolting and riveting the pieces together, connecting harnesses of electric wires and control systems, attaching the props, and turning down the landing gear. Once workers completed and inspected it, the Superfortress rolled out the door and entered flight test.

The multiline system had other advantages. The single-line system would have required more than fifty stations along the line. And the thousands of interior installations on the B-29—its wires and equipment—would have to be made after workers completed the fuselage and wings, which would have been very difficult, cramped, and slow work. Since the multiline system was really a series of systems, it was much easier to introduce changes in B-29 production as the experiences of flight and combat made them necessary. The different subassembly areas and teams of workers could be more easily rearranged under the multiline system. The long assembly line for autos was much less flexible—and could afford to be, since annual models of cars and trucks were generally exactly alike.

Multiline assembly also meant the plant could be built more efficiently and less expensively because a factory's exterior walls enclosed more floor space when arranged in big squares or near-square rectangles instead of long and narrow rectangles. And that meant that parts wouldn't have to be moved around in the plant over such long distances.

Such a straightforward description of B-29 multiline assembly gives a false sense of simplicity, however. The photos and the floor plan of Wichita suggest how complicated things actually were but hardly capture the real scene on the floor. At peak production during the daytime shift, close to 12,000 to 15,000 men and women worked in the plant.

Constant movement defined the plant floor as parts and materials went up and down, back and forth and across again on cranes, hoists, dollies, or in the arms of workers. The B-29 needed 40,540 different parts, not including duplicate parts, bolts, or the more than 1 million rivets. Imagine trying to follow, let alone plan, a system on the scale of a B-29 plant—a system that made sure everything got to the right place at the right time. One writer didn't exaggerate when he called the B-29 program "the greatest coordinated manufacturing enterprise in the history of American industry."

In the forming and machine shops, the air thundered with the sounds of giant presses coming down on aluminum stock to shape the sheet metal and extrusion lengths into parts. Big drilling machines made holes for rivets, screws, and bolts while cutting machines noisily sliced pieces of sheet or milled out structural metal into just the right shape.

In the assembly and subassembly areas, a constant piercing noise ripped around as thousands of compressed air guns pounded rivets tightly into place. Riveters made up 20 percent of the plant's workforce. By 1943, the majority of riveters were women. They worked in pairs, a riveter and a bucker. The riveter placed the rivet through the hole in the pieces of metal and held the air gun against its head. The bucker pushed a steel bar against the rivet's end on the other side and held it there until the air gun's action formed a mushroom of metal that was almost like a weld.

Riveting at Boeing–Renton. Courtesy of the Boeing Company (T56).

At work with a suspended riveter on the B-29's structural heart—the main wing spar. Although the women are wearing safety togs they aren't wearing ear protection. It's not hard to imagine just how noisy driving rivets in aluminum could be. Courtesy of the Boeing Company (WR-C6).

B-29s Accepted by the Army Air Forces, Month by Month, 1943–45

	Wichita	Marietta	Omaha	Renton	Total
1943					
July	7				7
August	4				4
September	15				15
October	13				13
November	17	1			18
December	31	3	1		35
Total	87	4	1		92
1944					
January	46	4	2		52
February	47	6	2		55
March	51	5	0	4	60
Apri	36	12	0	3	51
May	65	19	1	3	88
June	64	10	3	5	82
July	64	1	2	8	75
August	61	11	7	15	94
September	63	29	10	20	122
October	70	27	16	12	125
November	75	34	24	30	163
December	80	43	32	35	190
Total	722	201	99	135	1,161
1945					
January	86	45	40	50	221
February	100	50	50	60	260
March	100	56	55	80	291
April	105	61	55	100	321
May	95	60	55	140	350
June	100	65	55	150	370
July	100	60	55	160	375
August	100	50	50	119	319
September	37	16	21	52	126
October	2	—	—	—	2
November	—	—	—	3	3
December	—	—	—	4	4
Total	825	463	436	918	2,642
Grand total	1,634	668	536	1,057	3,895

Riveting and bucking were noisy, demanding jobs. The air gun and steel bar got heavier as the shift wore on. The work was very noisy, and in those days, factory workers rarely wore ear protection, which meant that many went home with ringing in their ears or headaches that kept them awake at night. The work was mentally draining, too, because it was so repetitive. It was boring but needed constant attention. Rivets had to be cleanly and tightly installed and the metal around them could not be damaged. And workers had to be careful not to injure themselves. Still, most workers put the best face on their jobs. "The riveter's job has a kick to it," said one young Wichita woman. "When you rivet those big pieces of skin on the plane you can see the bomber take shape before your eyes."

RENTON AND SEATTLE: "THE BIG CHANGE"

The B-29 plant in Renton, Washington, was another huge plant built by the government through the Defense Plant Corporation, about eight miles from Boeing's main works in Seattle on the south shore of Lake Washington. Planners originally expected that big Navy patrol planes would be built there. But in the summer of 1942, workers began converting Renton for B-29s. The Navy agreed to turn it over to the Army Air Forces in exchange for B-24 Liberator and B-25 Mitchell medium bombers from other plants.

The main factory extended 1,100 by 900 feet and covered 1.7 million square feet, including balconies. Final cost to the taxpayer for B-29 capital investment alone was $22.5 million. Government officials also had to spend $2.5 million to build runways alongside the plant. The Navy seaplanes would have taken off from the water. But B-29s needed thick, long, expensive concrete runways. Planners thought about moving the B-29s by barge to the air base at Sand's Point, but decided to build a new runway instead, which, like the plant, is still used by the Boeing Company.

Production planning for Renton B-29s began in July 1942. Planners hoped the first B-29 would fly a year later, in July 1943, and that output would reach thirty-five per month. As it turned out, the first Renton B-29 flew in January 1944. B-29 production at Renton suffered long delays and never filled expectations. The problem wasn't just Renton's late go-ahead, almost a year and a half after Wichita's. Severe shortages of aluminum and other materials also caused problems. More important was the shortage of personnel— engineers, managers, and especially workers. The plant at Renton was underutilized and poorly managed, its production quota continually downscaled.

Stiff competition for personnel at Renton came from Boeing–Seattle operating all-out for B-17 production in 1942. The Army couldn't get enough Flying Fortresses for the air war in Europe and kept insisting on design changes that took up a lot of engineers' time. Also, defense work swamped the Seattle–Tacoma area. The Navy and Maritime Commission had big orders for warships and transports with local shipyards. And, to the east, in Hanford, Washington, a huge construction project for the atomic bomb program also absorbed many workers, men and women offered $1.00 an hour plus travel costs just to be "day-laborers" on the top secret Manhattan Project.

The government tagged Seattle–Tacoma a "critical labor area" in 1943. This meant too many jobs went begging for too few workers in King, Kitsap, and Pierce counties. It was definitely a seller's market for workers and a big change from the Depression years. At Boeing, the problems of labor shortages were compounded because aircraft workers' pay was 25 percent lower than in other defense industries, a serious handicap for the company trying to attract and keep workers. Boeing and the local shipyards both had huge demands for new workers who could do unskilled or semi-skilled work. But starting pay at the shipyards was 95 cents an hour. At Boeing it was 67 cents, rising to only 75 cents after three months on the job. Many workers naturally chose the shipyards.

Boeing also had a bad image in Seattle as an employer during these years, which just added to the low-wage problem in workers' minds. Boeing's problems stemmed from the company's experiences with its men and the federal government during the late 1930s and early 1940s. Until 1941 and the use of cost-plus contracts, the aircraft industry was very competitive. Companies bid against each other for Army, Navy, and airline contracts, which led to heavy downward pressure on wages, since workers' pay made up more than half the cost involved in the labor-intensive process of building planes. Boeing's problem was especially bad because relatively high wages were the norm in the Seattle–Tacoma area. Boeing's main competitors—Douglas, Lockheed, North American, and Consolidated—operated in low-wage Southern California.

To stay competitive Boeing had to keep its wage bills down. But complaints from poorly paid workers increased. In 1940, they voted in new leaders for their union, the International Association of Machinists, Lodge #751. They demanded better pay and working conditions, but the company stalled. It was already losing money on its contracts, which it had signed on a fixed-price basis. Boeing could not attract new investors. Only a loan guarantee from a New Deal agency kept the firm solvent. Even worse for labor organizers at Boeing, most Americans had come to believe that Communists

or "subversives," trying to prevent the United States from rearming, stirred up such labor complaints and strikes—even when they were due to genuine hardship among workers. Powerful people in Seattle and Washington, D.C., worked to get Lodge #751's militant leaders fired.

The Seattle police and city council, local newspapers, the Machinists' national leaders in Washington, D.C., and officials of the FBI, the War Department, and the White House all finally succeeded in the spring of 1941. Investigations were launched into "communistic connections at the Boeing plant." No significant evidence was found, but the new union leaders were ousted and the union basically broken. A strong United Auto Worker local union in Los Angeles aircraft was also broken in 1941. For the most part, organized unions remained very weak and outside the planning, management, and wage-setting loops throughout the wartime aircraft industry.

Boeing workers felt bitter about how their collective-bargaining rights had been violated. The company's difficulties in hiring new workers did not improve. Federal government officials kept a tight lid on pay for aircraft workers through the war years. Since aircraft workers made up the biggest share of people doing military work, government officials feared that wage increases in aircraft would fuel national price inflation. And after Pearl Harbor, union leaders made a "no-strike pledge" for the war's duration, which meant there was no effective way for workers to press for better wages.

Even though they generally regarded aircraft work as lighter and more interesting than other work, and even though it was inside and out of the weather, workers weren't attracted to Boeing. Through 1942–44, managers struggled to find enough people to keep up their B-17 production quotas and to start turning out B-29s from Renton.

Boeing managers faced very high labor turnover rates—over 100 percent. This meant that in any given period as many people quit working for Boeing as the company hired, a wasteful and frustrat-

Der Fuehrer's Face

THE commander of a unit attacking a military objective is always glad if he finds the enemy's position weak or undefended because the enemy failed to get or keep enough soldiers on the job at that particular point. In a war in which the production of weapons is so important, the opposing forces can be just as happy when the enemy fails to get, or keep, enough workers in the factories.

Every time one of our workers is absent, it means a loss, to us, of at least eight manhours. A thousand absences in a day (and there are *always* more than a thousand absent at Boeing *every* day) equals at least 8000 man-hours. It doesn't take long at that rate, to lose a Flying Fortress that might have been built but wasn't.

Since the fewer Boeing B-17s we have the better Hitler likes it, the mere thought of our absentee employees makes him grin. As our absentee rate goes down, so do the corners of Der Fuehrer's mouth.

This effect of attendance on Der Fuehrer's face will be graphically illustrated in all Boeing shops and departments from now on. The four faces at the left are a cross-section of expressions, one of which will appear in each department's poster according to the previous day's attendance record. Hitler will be hilarious at more than ten percent absence. He'll howl with grief only when the department hits the irreducible minimum of absentees. And, in between those extremes, he'll be smug or doubtful or gloomy, as the case may be.

So, let's keep the smile off Der Fuehrer's face!

Der Fuehrer's Face...

...REFLECTS Yesterday's Absentees

SHOP 399

MEN	0
WOMEN	0
SHOP AVERAGE	0
FACTORY AVERAGE	2.6

A regular feature in the *Boeing News* as part of the effort to combat absenteeism among aircraft workers in Seattle. Courtesy of the Boeing Company (*Boeing News,* April 1943).

"Are YOU Pitching with BOTH HANDS Brother?"

GET A WAR JOB!

A poster put up in aircraft plants to try to appeal to workers' consciences in the battle against absenteeism. This veteran has lost both his hands in combat. Courtesy of the National Archives.

Women working on B-29 wiring assemblies in a storefront window in the old McDermott Building at 2nd Street and Union in downtown Seattle as part of Boeing's recruitment campaign. The idea was to encourage women to go to work on B-29s. Courtesy of the Boeing Company (P3339).

ing situation. The Army and Navy drafted many young Boeing workers. But the main reason was that workers preferred working elsewhere. Many learned basic skills at Boeing, only to move on to other jobs where the pay was better.

Boeing also had a big problem with workers who didn't show up at the plant when they were supposed to. Like high turnover rates, high absenteeism—sometimes as much as 10 percent a shift—reflected worker resentment with low wages and poor relations with management. It reflected as well the simple fact that people got sick and couldn't go to work. And some people didn't care, were lazy, or knew they could always get another job if they got fired.

As early as 1943, many people thought that the war was practically over. Reports poured in of victories over the Germans, especially by the Soviets on the Eastern Front. And Americans made steady progress against the Japanese in the Pacific. For many workers, the smart move seemed to be out of the aircraft plants, which they thought would close at war's end, to get a head start in jobs with a postwar future.

Another cause of turnover and absenteeism was the plain difficulty of aircraft workers' lives in Seattle. With all the aircraft and shipyard jobs, the population exploded in numbers as people poured in from outlying areas and from out of state. There weren't enough houses and apartments or ways to get to work. The roads to the Boeing plant were jammed with cars and it was hard to find parking spaces. Women had trouble finding babysitters, day-care, doctors, and places to shop.

One federal official warned in the summer of 1943 that "the community is dangerously unprepared to absorb the in-migration" of tens of thousands of people. Many residents of Seattle, including newspaper editors, blamed Boeing for lack of foresight and poor management. They wrote to Washington, D.C., complaining about "the magnitude of the operations at Boeing, and the lack of personnel engineering," which "brought about the present deterioration of morale and are preventing efficient operation of the organization."

Despite its many problems, Boeing still managed to find enough people. Workers built some 3,600 B-17s, and spare parts, by November 1943, about the time when the "Big Change" was begun—the shift to B-29 production. The numbers of B-17s were below plans but still an accomplishment, due in part to Boeing's ability to keep a core of experienced supervisors and foremen, many of whom received special exemptions from the draft.

The government also helped Boeing. In June 1943, Undersecretary of War Robert Patterson ordered no new defense contracts for the Seattle area unless cleared by him. And a special group of Army labor relations experts was ordered into Boeing during the summer by worried officials in the White House and War Department. They pushed through some small pay increases and showed Boeing how to build better relations with workers by consulting with the union and with people on the factory floor.

These experts also found new ways to train workers faster and new ways to break down and simplify the work so it became even easier for the inexperienced. Leading citizens of the community were asked to help recruit people and improve Boeing's image in the Seattle area. The planners showed Boeing how to handle the explosion in its workforce and be a more progressive, sophisticated employer. Planners also took pressure off the Seattle plants by using government funds to start branch plants for B-17 subassemblies in the Puget Sound area which were later converted to B-29 parts. "Feeder" factories opened in Bellingham, Everett, Aberdeen, Chehalis; two opened in Tacoma.

But Boeing managed to perform as well as it did mainly because of the women hired in large numbers beginning in 1942. In March 1942, women made up only 2 percent of Boeing's direct workforce. By August 1944, 41,564 people worked for Boeing in Seattle and Renton. Of these, 13,567 worked white-collar, pink-collar, or indirect jobs. They were the executives, managers, engineers, office staff, supervisors, foremen, janitors, and guards. Those who worked directly with their hands on aircraft numbered 23,257. Another

Final assembly station at the Renton plant. Courtesy of the Boeing Company (X346).

Bomb-bay preparations at Renton. In the foreground, he rivets while she handles the buck. Women made up the majority of "productive" workers, those who performed actual manufacturing tasks, a consistent pattern throughout America's wartime aircraft industry. Courtesy of the Boeing Company (X330).

Inspecting lower dorsal fins for delivery to Renton and final B-29 assembly. Courtesy of the Boeing Company (X361).

Stabilizers at Boeing's Seattle plant for delivery to Renton. Such images are visually impressive but indicate an imbalance or bottleneck in B-29 production. Courtesy of the Boeing Company (X360).

5,500 or so worked in the subassembly feeder plants. About 54 percent of these productive workers were women of ages anywhere between 16 and 65 years. They did unskilled and semi-skilled jobs, like riveting, bucking, inspection, and feeding aluminum into cutting and stamping machines. Without women, multiline assembly of B-17s and B-29s would have come to a standstill. At Renton, about 7,500 people worked on B-29s in August 1944, the month that deceleration of B-17 production began. Most were women. About 2,550 women and 2,010 men held direct production jobs. Another 2,900—mainly women—became "paper shufflers," filling indirect jobs at desks on the factory floor or in the offices.

Planners eased workers' lives by staggering shifts, which cut congestion on the roads, parking lots, buses, and at the entrance gates. The first shift's start was split between 6:30 and 7:30 in the morning. It ended when the second shift began between 3:00 and 4:00 in the afternoon. The small cleanup, maintenance, and planning staff on the third shift came in at 11:30 P.M. and 12:30 A.M. Federal officials also financed and built Boeing Town near the Renton factory, a new community offering 3,000 housing, apartment, and dormitory units. Boeing Town, with its new busing, shopping, recreation, health care, and day-care facilities, helped relieve "unhealthy" living conditions for workers and made employment at Renton much more attractive.

Still, Renton B-29 production faced shortages of some 4,000 workers in September 1944. They were needed to bring output to the levels planned and to offset the still-high quit and absentee rates. These shortages made failure of planned B-29 production schedules inevitable and helped keep the plant months behind Wichita in placing into initial production the B-29's endless stream of design changes and modifications. At the modification center in Denver, it always took longer to modify Renton B-29s and get them ready for combat.

"The local pool of labor has been pretty much exhausted," complained one Army official in the summer of 1944, adding that "there

is a definite 'war is over' trend," thanks to so many Allied victories, especially after D day in Europe. It was widely assumed that Nazi Germany would collapse in September or October 1944. Boeing could not guarantee workers postwar jobs. Many quit, thinking they ought "to get out of the war job" and get a head start on jobs with a future.

It is worth noting that the rights of people to work where they wanted were never violated by the government through "compulsory job controls" or conscription. Local officials had federal authority to give defense companies "priorities" in hiring, and Boeing got a top rating. But officials never used their power "because of the futility of trying to hold a discontented employee." Also, the government never forced Boeing workers to do ten-hour shifts even though the company strongly insisted on it and pointed to how successful it was in Wichita. The workers and their union opposed the ten-hour shift, arguing that it would be too tiring and lead to even lower productivity than the eight-hour shift. They pointed out that workers' lives were much easier in Wichita and that wages there went much further.

Planners never solved the problem of labor shortages at Renton. But the pressure was relieved somewhat as the men and women became more efficient and productive and as the Big Change took effect. Planners wound down B-17 work at the various Boeing plants along Puget Sound and replaced it with B-29 work. At Plant 2, a $17.5-million B-17 plant built by the government at Boeing's home base on East Marginal Way, the replacement of B-17 production equipment by jigs and machines for B-29s happened like a slowly moving wave across the plant's 1.7 million square–foot floor. Planners called it "an industrial squeezeplay."

"Feeder plants" that had been sending B-17 parts to Plant 2 in Seattle now made B-29 subassemblies for Renton. And new feeders were set up especially for Superfortress assemblies. Another one went up in Everett, and two more in Hoquiam. Some 7,500 Canadians, mostly women, built bomb-bay sections for Renton 150

Preparing the tail gunner's cabin windshield at a feeder plant in Hoquiam, Washington, for delivery to Renton. Courtesy of the Boeing Company (P5602).

Boeing workers take the sun among the houses, trees, and streets of the fake neighborhood built on top of Boeing Plant 2 in Seattle. The military hoped this detailed camouflage would fool enemy bombers. After Pearl Harbor, it seemed to most everyone in the Seattle area that they, too, might be open to air attack. Courtesy of the Boeing Company (P5856).

miles away at the old Boeing seaplane plant along the mouth of the Fraser River in Vancouver, British Columbia. Every day, in late 1944 and early 1945, Vancouver bomb bays rolled across the Canadian border to Renton for final assembly.

Planners also relieved pressure on Renton by increasing the amount of B-29 parts made by other companies on subcontracts. In 1944, subcontracted parts—not including subassemblies—made up about 13 percent of a Renton B-29's weight. By 1945, the figure had grown to 25 percent. Most of these Boeing–Renton subcontracts were filled by companies in western Washington, Oregon, Idaho, and British Columbia. Others were filled by manufacturing companies across the nation. It is hard to give a figure for the number of people who worked on these B-29 subcontracts and those of the three other B-29 plants. But they are just as important to the story of "who built the B-29?"

Still, planners were regularly obliged to scale down Renton's production schedule, which shook up Army Air Force plans to train B-29 crews and drop bombs on Japan. Plans for the B-29 had to be cut back because 498 of them weren't going to be built on time. "This reduction in the number of B-29s to be made tactically available" one planner wrote, "is almost wholly a result of the reduction in the latest estimate of B-29s to be delivered by Boeing–Renton." Gen. Oliver Echols complained at a meeting of the Air Staff (the high command of the Army Air Forces) that an "adjustment" had to be made "in the entire B-29 program" because of the "failure of the Boeing–Seattle–Renton facility to meet its schedule."

In the 12-month period from October 1944 to September 1945, Renton was supposed to build 1,535 B-29s worth nearly $700 million. But the quota was cut to 1,065. Even then, planners had their doubts, "in view of the confusion at Boeing–Renton." Renton more and more became just a point for final assembly, producing hardly any of the spare parts that the other plants turned out. Only the wing's center section was built at Renton.

The situation at Boeing was complicated even more by the sudden death in November 1944 of Philip G. Johnson, the company's president. His steady hand had guided the firm through all the challenges and frustrations of suddenly becoming a major employer and a reliable supplier of large and very advanced aircraft. By July 1945, Renton workers were assembling 160 B-29s per month! This was more than any of the other three factories, but, of course, many fewer B-29 components were produced there and Renton B-29s needed more time at the modification centers. Employment at all Boeing facilities around Seattle peaked in February 1945 at 45,008 men and women. On August 14, 1945—V-J day—35,652 men and women worked on B-29s and on other Boeing projects, such as the C-97 cargo plane, the B-50 heavy bomber, the Stratocruiser airliner, and the new jet-engine, swept-wing medium bomber XB-47. Employment fell steadily after V-J day, even though the plan was to continue turning out B-29s for the postwar air force.

Suddenly, on September 5, 1945, the government canceled all new B-29 work at Renton and would accept only those already in the production pipeline. More than 21,000 people were laid off overnight, causing much dislocation and anxiety for Boeing workers. The feeder plants were closed and by the end of the month, only 8,400 Boeing employees remained. In the end, Boeing workers in the Pacific Northwest turned out 1,037 B-29s.

OMAHA

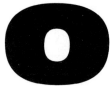maha, Nebraska, seemed a good place to build a giant new aircraft factory for the same reasons that made Wichita a likely spot. Omaha had little of the long experience with aviation that Wichita had, but its distance from seacoasts and borders gave it the same strategic attractions. Many competent, hardworking but unemployed people lived near Omaha and across the Missouri River at Council Bluffs, Iowa. And, as planners noted, the area's labor pool featured mainly "native-born Americans," much like Wichita 330 miles away. It was assumed that "native-born Americans" could be counted on to eagerly fill the plants and do the work. They also were believed to be more patriotic, less likely to commit sabotage or be interested in unions that might demand higher pay and try to influence plant management, the way more ethnically diverse workers tended to in the nation's older manufacturing centers.

Omaha lobbyists and the Nebraska delegation to Congress aggressively argued these points in Washington, D.C. Led by the senior senator from Nebraska, George W. Norris, the group made its case at the White House. They went to FDR "to press the claims of this territory for national defense projects and industries." In December 1940, government officials announced that the Glenn L. Martin Company of Baltimore would manage a new complex south of Omaha and mass-produce its two-engine medium bomber, the B-26 Marauder. Company and government planners chose a site at old Fort Crook near the town of Bellevue in Sarpy County, Nebraska. It was well serviced by railroads and near a bridge across the Missouri.

Announcement of the new plant caused much local excitement, as it did wherever new aircraft plants went up in wartime America. Real estate speculators got to work as newspapers announced a "terrific housing boom." "Residents Cheer Bomber Plant as Pointing to Boom," read one newspaper headline. Local boosters hailed the decision. "This appears to be the biggest thing since the packing industry came to Omaha," said an ecstatic W. C. Fraser, president of the Omaha Chamber of Commerce. He accurately predicted what the decision meant for Omaha's future as a permanent site for American air power.

The Army Corps of Engineers supervised site preparation and construction of the various buildings that made up Government

Aircraft Assembly Plant #1, Omaha. It eventually cost more than $20 million. The largest building was Plant D, a $10-million final assembly building with 1.2 million square feet of floor space. Plant D was a reverse copy of the Martin plant in Baltimore designed by Albert Kahn, the great industrial architect from Detroit.

At Fort Crook, a once-sleepy Army base, life swirled in the spring and summer of 1941. The 3,500 construction workers reshaped the landscape with giant bulldozers and Euclid tractors, all with Stars and Stripes snapping in the wind from rearview mirrors. The rolling hills needed 70 feet of excavation to create a level site and provide proper drainage. Workers then built wooden forms, poured concrete, and erected steel for state-of-the-art buildings, new runways, parking lots, and a "superhighway" to Omaha.

They finished construction in October 1941. But delays in finding and setting up machine tools and jigs plagued the Martin works through 1942. Only in August 1942 did the plant's first B-26 fly away and only in December did the plant achieve its scheduled production. Then, a few months later, talk of converting the factory to B-29 production began. The B-26 was much criticized in the national media and by congressmen and Army officers. Its high-powered engines and narrow wings made it a "hot plane," even a "vicious plane," in the minds of some pilots. In the hands of experienced fliers, the Marauder could be a lethal and effective weapon. But for the many young pilots in training and just beginning their careers, the B-26 was very hard to handle. Too many B-26 crashes killed too many crewmen, so the Army Air Forces decided to cut back on the B-26 and the negative publicity it generated.

In July 1943, the Army Air Forces began phasing out B-26s at Omaha. Planners rearranged the plant and its subcontracting network to build the B-29, which one local newspaper described as "the most powerful weapon mankind has ever built." Workers would prepare center wing sections from scratch at Martin–Omaha, but the plant, like Boeing–Renton, was basically a final assembly center for B-29 components made elsewhere. Chrysler supplied nose sections, nacelles, leading edges, and center wing flaps at its plants in Detroit and sent them by rail to Omaha. Goodyear, in Akron, Ohio, built bomb-bay fuselage sections and Hudson Motor of Detroit provided fuselage waist sections and tail gun turrets. And J. I. Case, the tractor and farm equipment–maker, supplied outer wing panels, wing tips and ailerons, and tail parts—the dorsal fin, the vertical fin, and the rudder.

By October 1943, officers committed $90 million to Martin–Omaha to convert its jigs, dies, and tools for B-29 final assembly and to buy material. That was a rough figure because, as one AAF contracting officer put it, "negotiations covering the entire procurement will be initiated upon the final determination of the details" and "as the engineering details of the Omaha Program unfold."

The plan was to deliver the first B-29 in June 1944 and accelerate to an output of twenty B-29s per month by August. Actual first delivery, however, came a month sooner, in May 1944, a month after the last Omaha B-26 was built, for a total of 1,536 B-26s. In June, the Army Air Forces ordered the "acceleration of B-29 airplanes at Martin" because good progress by Martin–Nebraska workers "warrant a step-up of their schedule." Martin managers and workers succeeded despite many of the familiar problems—constant design changes, material, equipment, and labor shortages—and despite other problems unique to the Omaha project.

For example, Martin kept building B-26s while workers converted the plant for B-29s, a situation that often led to much confusion. And changes had to be made to the factory's structure. Plant D's roof trusses were fine for B-26s, but too low for the B-29's towering tail. The trusses were raised, but rather than alter the main doors, tractors hauled B-29s out of the plant with their nosewheels jacked up three feet so the tail ducked down low enough to fit through.

A breakdown in trust and cooperation among Martin executives, AAF planners, and representatives of the various subcontractors caused many delays in the fall of 1943. Martin took over the Fisher

Company's B-29 contracts and commitments, but nearly half of Fisher's blueprints and data sheets proved so specialized that Martin engineers couldn't understand them. And Martin's subcontractors worried about their exposure to the B-29 program, especially during the general B-29 production crisis of the fall of 1943 when it looked like the whole undertaking might collapse. The subs insisted that their old contracts with Fisher not be transferred to Martin but rewritten instead so that they had better protection in "prime direct contracts from the government."

Army Air Force officers, impatient with B-29 delays, complained about the conservatism and "lack of leadership" by the Martin company. The company's reputation had suffered—unfairly—because of all the criticism of the B-26. It seemed that Martin executives stalled just to see how the overall B-29 program would be reorganized and whether it would even proceed. The generals bitterly complained about the endless "paper work" involved with transferring the Fisher contracts to Martin. They sneered at "these lawyers . . . seeing that all t's are crossed and all i's are dotted and the periods in the proper places and all that sort of thing." One general demanded that Martin executives "knock some people's heads together and get the thing going."

Knots were gradually undone as Martin executives and their subs received the assurances they demanded from the government and as men and women filled the plant to get B-29 production lines ready. In November 1943, employment peaked and leveled at about 14,500 workers, three-quarters of whom came from the Omaha–Council Bluffs area. Women made up 40 percent of the total. According to the Omaha World Herald, women especially enjoyed working at the plant and helping to "bring misery to Hitler, Hirohito, and the unhappy fascist." Contributing to the war effort served as a prime motivator for many workers, particularly those who had relatives and loved ones in the armed forces.

Martin workers succeeded because they enjoyed better and more encouraging working and living conditions than most else-where. The B-29's many delays could be demoralizing, especially in 1943. But since Martin started later than Wichita and Marietta, planners could avoid their mistakes and learn their lessons. Once B-29 production was rolling, a strong sense of accomplishment animated the Martin men and women. Most Martin workers were delighted when on May 24, 1944, the first Martin B-29, Satan's Angel, rolled out of Plant D.

Operations were smaller and less crowded than at other B-29 plants. And overall defense employment around Omaha was lower than in other locales. That meant demand for housing, child care, schools, recreation, shopping, medical care, and transportation was not as great. Aircraft wages went further and were relatively higher than other industries in Omaha. And federal social agencies cooperated better and coordinated their work more effectively with local groups like the Chamber of Commerce, all in an effort to make workers' lives easier.

The U.S. Employment Service and National Youth Administration worked with local high schools, vocational schools, and the company to train workers for aircraft. Together, they provided 450,000 training hours during the switch from the B-26 to the B-29 alone. Thousands of mostly teenagers and young men and women developed new skills at Martin that they used to contribute to the area's economy for the rest of their lives.

Luella Johnson said she "didn't know a screwdriver from a crescent wrench." She had been selling dresses in a women's store but took training for a key role in B-29 final assembly. Mary Duncan waited on tables in Falls City, Nebraska. After a six-week course, she worked a turret lathe at Martin. Generally, women did better at Martin–Nebraska than elsewhere in aircraft. They received pay and had opportunities on the same scale as men and took up more responsible positions. Many ingredients helped make successful an operation as complicated as a B-29 factory. But few were as important as conditions that made all workers feel as though they could contribute to the best of their ability.

The *Enola Gay* on its return from Hiroshima. Courtesy of the National Air and Space Museum, Smithsonian Institution (AC-59476).

Bocks Car was built in Omaha. Its nose art was painted on by the crew and refers to the pilot's home in Utah. Courtesy of the National Air and Space Museum, Smithsonian Institution (AC-39807).

Workers felt little need for a union. The United Auto Workers, a leading national union, managed to win recognition as collective-bargaining agent for Martin–Nebraska workers only after much legal action and despite the workers' apathy. The UAW won a key election in early 1945, but only five months before the plant closed down because of Japan's surrender.

By early 1945, Martin workers turned out fifty-five B-29s per month. These needed many fewer modifications than B-29s from the other plants. Military investigators gave the plant the highest marks for "quality control." And the Army Air Forces selected Martin–Omaha for Silver Plate, the secret project to specially modify B-29s for carrying atomic bombs. Omaha workers built *Enola Gay* and *Bocks Car*, the B-29s that struck Hiroshima and Nagasaki on August 6 and 9, 1945.

Workers continued turning out B-29s, building parts, and modifying B-29s from other plants through the summer of 1945. They kept it up, even though many quit to get married, have children, go back to the farm, or simply because of "general restlessness," as one report put it. By war's end, Martin workers built 536 Superfortresses, about 14 percent of the total. All of these, according to local newswriters, "are plastering the Japanese homeland."

The end for B-29 production at Martin came suddenly. Within 30 days of V-J day, 15,000 people lost their jobs. Plant D was mothballed and became a storage center for the government's surplus machine tools. It is now part of Offut Air Force Base, which served until early 1991 as headquarters for the former U.S. Air Force Strategic Air Command.

MARIETTA, GEORGIA

Two weeks after the Japanese attacked Pearl Harbor on December 7, 1941, Gen. Henry "Hap" Arnold called Larry Bell, president of the Bell Aircraft Company of Buffalo, New York, asking him to join the B-29 program. Bell was one of the nation's most admired aircraft designers and executives. The industry as a whole had trouble meeting big commitments to build large numbers of warplanes for the Army and Navy and for the Allies. But Bell Aircraft was ahead of its schedules in Buffalo. The company turned out P-39 Airacobra fighters. Larry Bell even found time to represent the aircraft industry on an important government board that made national policy on how the industry's problems—especially with aircraft workers—should be handled. Bell was broadminded and not afraid to think big. He seemed ideal for B-29 work, especially for running one of the program's most ambitious parts—the enormous new B-29 plant planned for Atlanta. However, as things turned out, the new plant proved too ambitious even for Larry Bell and his company.

Bell and his executives moved quickly on the B-29 and with plenty of confidence. On New Year's Day 1942, Bell flew to Seattle with men from Fisher to discuss the project with the Boeing people. A week later, a team of Bell managers and lawyers went to Atlanta to look at possible plant sites and to gather estimates on land, construction, equipment, and labor costs. Bell agreed to set up the plant and build B-29s under a cost-plus-fixed-fee deal. In other words, the company hired out its management skills to the government. When the plant was finished, the company used it under an operating lease.

Why Atlanta? The city was not the first choice for a new government aircraft assembly plant; in fact, it was one of the last. Big government plants had been going up across the country since France fell in the summer of 1940 but the decision to go with Atlanta was made only after Pearl Harbor. There had been much talk about Georgia's getting a good scoop out of what some called the aircraft industry "pork barrel." And for years, Franklin Roosevelt's New Deal administration had tried to find ways to jumpstart and modernize the South's depressed economy—the "Nation's Number One Problem."

But planners feared that aircraft plants in Georgia would be too close to the Gulf and Atlantic coasts and too easily open to air attack. Georgia was not selected early on even though some of the most powerful figures in Congress were from Georgia, including senators Walter George and Richard Russell, and Congressman Carl Vinson, the chairman of the House Naval Affairs Committee, who had long experience with the aircraft industry. These Georgia representatives sensed the apparent risks of building key aircraft plants back home. Commenting at the time of the Nazi air raids on the Dutch city of Rotterdam, Senator George told a reporter that "I would like to see aircraft plants in Georgia, but feel that we must take into consideration their protection and for this decision I am content to rely upon the Army and Navy. . . . This is a matter about which we must be scientific rather than political."

By the time of Pearl Harbor, a year and a half later, few inland sites remained that could provide the kind of workforce big aircraft plants needed. The decision to go with Atlanta with Government Aircraft Assembly Plant #6 was based on what looked like a good reserve of people who could go to work, a consideration that offset the strategic dangers. Bell executives agreed that a large section of land in Cobb County was the best choice, 20 miles northwest of Atlanta near the town of Marietta and Kennesaw Mountain, site of the last major stand of the Confederate Army against Sherman's March during the Civil War. Officers of the site selection committee of the Army Corps of Engineers picked Marietta because of the low costs of land, the main rail line that ran through town, and the fact that plenty of unemployed people lived in the area. The Corps of Engineers also oversaw construction of the plant and its equipment on behalf of the Defense Plant Corporation. Here, B-29 planners made one of the most important decisions for the economic history of Georgia and the South. This huge complex, with its floor area of 3.9 million square feet, still employs thousands as one of the nation's few remaining military-aircraft assembly plants.

The Army Air Forces mothballed Plant 6 after the war, but Lockheed Corporation reopened it during the Korean War. Since then, it has been an anchor for well-paying aerospace jobs and the development of a high-technology industrial base in the South. Lockheed built B-47 bombers and hundreds of big military air transports at Marietta—the C-130 Hercules, the C-141 Starlifter, and the C-5 Galaxy. Plant 6 is expected to turn out the next generation of jet fighters—the Lockheed F-22.

In January 1945, General Wolfe summed up Plant 6, telling the people of Marietta that "this plant is not merely the greatest industrial installation of the Deep South, it is one of the great industrial installations of the world. . . . It will serve the industrialization program of our Southern States in the postwar era." The general had to be hoping that Plant 6 would perform better in the postwar world than it did on the B-29. If the Superfortresses hadn't performed so well burning out Japanese cities and had they not been credited with ending the Second World War by dropping atomic bombs on Hiroshima and Nagasaki, Bell–Marietta might have been something of a scandal.

No big thinking, grand visions, or costs were spared at Marietta. Planners set initial production schedules very optimistically, pegging delivery of the first Bell B-29 in September 1943—only twenty-two months away. They hoped for a running output of 65 B-29s a month by June 1944 for a total of 700 B-29s by January 1945. Bell would build its center wing sections, all fuselage pieces, and most installations. The company agreed to build 69 percent of its B-29 parts and components and even send some subassemblies to the other B-29 plants.

In mid-February 1942, Bell executives and engineers, who were used to small, compact fighters, toured Boeing–Wichita and some big B-17 and B-24 plants in Texas and California. They concluded that the Marietta schedule had to be scaled back to 40 B-29s per month, with a total output of 400. Even then, everyone agreed that the Bell program was "terrifically ambitious." To meet the schedule, production would have to begin by January 1, 1943. This meant that the factory would have to be practically complete, workers available and trained, assembly lines laid out, and machine tools, jigs, and fixtures built and installed—all in less than eleven months and at a time when detailed engineering and tooling data for the B-29 was still very scarce and vague and when serious shortages of steel, aluminum, and machine tools plagued the nation's war economy.

Officials pushed on anyway. At the end of March 1942, workers broke ground and began excavations for Plant 6. The Corps of Engineers hired Robert & Company to manage plant design and construction. At first, planners thought Bell needed a building with floorspace of 2,200,000 square feet. That figure was soon bumped to an enormous 3,955,800 square feet. Plant 6 turned out to be very expensive to build and operate. By 1944, $47 million in federal funds had gone into the plant, its equipment, and the runways. It had to be a "blackout plant" because lights would be targets for enemy planes. This meant no windows, no natural ventilation, and costly air conditioning and fluorescent lighting. The builders promised they would have some of the plant ready for production gear by September 1942.

Working a seven-day week mainly back in Buffalo, Bell engineers and consultants began planning the layout and designing jigs, fixtures, and tools. They agreed to work with the B-29 liaison committee based in Seattle. In May 1942, the War Department officially approved Bell's $342-million contract for 400 B-29s and spares by January 1945. But everyone knew this schedule would not be met. Despite all the furious construction activity at Marietta, it was obvious that Plant 6 would not be finished until March or April of 1943, and the runways not until July 1943.

By the end of June 1942, the building was only 3 percent complete. Bethlehem Steel couldn't fill orders for Plant 6's 32,000 tons of structural steel because of national shortages. Planners pushed back the plant's completion date and Bell executives started fretting about how they might have bitten off more than they could chew. They tried to scale back their promises for supplying components to the others. They also faced serious difficulties in the simple fact that the B-29 was not yet an airplane. The XB-29 didn't fly until September 1942.

Bell executives couldn't know just what they had contracted to build. The aircraft was still in design, and the Boeing Company fell well behind its promise to supply the master-gauges and photo-templates for the tools, presses, and cutting machines that made the B-29's tens of thousands of parts. The guides were supposed to have been sent to Bell by June 1942. Bell didn't even have data on the main wing spar or the official bill of material that showed how much of what material and which parts had to be ordered. In June 1942, plant layout at Marietta was only 10 percent complete. Hard feelings developed among executives from Bell, Boeing, and the other companies on the B-29 liaison committee. Some complained about "confusion" and the "lack of engineering information." They insisted that Boeing find more people for B-29 engineering and that the "constant changes" be "more efficiently planned."

The military began blaming Bell for the delays. The Army Corps of Engineers insisted that the 700 Bell engineers designing B-29 tools and jigs in Buffalo be moved south to the site at Marietta and that more of them be hired. Impatience with the company grew as Bell asked to have its first delivery date pushed back to December 1943. Riggers set the last piece of structural steel into place in January 1943. But "muddy and dusty" Plant 6 was far from ready. By March, some 5,000 construction workers had the plant 90 percent complete, but only 3,000 men—mostly from Buffalo—worked on B-29 tooling and production. In an attempt to meet the original schedule for first delivery, some of them worked to build a single B-29, casting and hammering out its parts by hand because so little of the tooling and machinery was ready.

Many of Bell's top executives moved from New York to Atlanta "to get the project rolling." Experts from Detroit production engineering companies were hired. Still, Plant 6 had only 40 percent of its production equipment in place in March 1943. Engineering

View of construction scaffolding at Plant 6 in Marietta. The plant used up nearly 2 billion pounds of construction materials. Now operating under the Lockheed name, the building itself is one of the few tangible legacies of the hundreds of millions of dollars spent at the plant during the war. Less than a handful of B-29s still survive, the rest were destroyed or scrapped. Courtesy Atlanta History Center (BLL-1-32).

changes on the B-29 came from Boeing at a steady and rapid rate, disrupting the plant's tooling-up. And even basic machinery and equipment couldn't be bought anywhere because of the huge demand throughout America's war industry. All in all, Bell fell five months behind its already extended schedule.

During the spring and fall of 1943 it seemed the whole B-29 project would collapse. For everyone involved with the Superfortress those months were a time of anxiety, even despair. B-29 planners singled out Boeing for blame, citing its delays in providing reliable data for B-29 production. They also pointed at Curtiss-Wright's failures with the R-3350 engine. But Bell, too, came in for much criticism. To outside observers, it seemed that Bell managers and workers wasted time and energy tooling up Marietta. Bell engineers used an old-fashioned tooling system called "lofting," a time-consuming way of transferring data from blueprints and spec sheets to the metal presses and cutting machines that made B-29 parts. Bell draftsmen drew B-29 parts and pieces in full size on giant sheets of paper. These were then photographed and reproduced on metal templates, cut out, and installed in the machinery.

Boeing executives, and others in the B-29 liaison committee, insisted that Bell use copies of the templates already made at Wichita. They claimed that Bell's process kept tooling at Marietta months behind schedule, mainly because it was so hard to find qualified draftsmen. Meanwhile, delays at Marietta prompted federal officials in the War Production Board to downgrade Bell's priority claims on the nation's limited aluminum and steel supplies. One Bell executive worried about how this move "will keep the Bell plant practically empty for a year."

Bell executives stubbornly insisted that their system was better, that it made things easier for training new workers. They warned that "if we are forced to give up lofting, we would not guarantee performance. . . . In our contract, the method to be employed was left entirely to our discretion." Bell's lofting and tooling-up went on. Planners decided that an attempt had to be made to get at least the first Bell B-29s as close to schedule as possible. They agreed that the first few would be made mainly with parts and components supplied by Wichita. These parts, it was hoped, would also help engineers and workers get a better sense of what they were doing. But Bell workers discovered, much to everyone's shock, that the circumferences of the first fuselage sections to arrive from Wichita were "out of tolerance" with those built in Marietta.

Still, progress was slowly made. In July 1943, an XB-29 landed at Marietta, offering "the first time that Bell's people had an opportunity to see one of these ships." All involved also took great delight in the first flight of a Wichita B-29. Plant 6 neared 100 percent completion and 70 percent of the tooling was in. The building amazed everyone who saw it. One writer said it seemed "as though one had suddenly come across the architecture of a people from another and larger planet." In Georgia's steamy July, a big day came when electricians finally turned on the air conditioning.

Army officers suggested that Bell let Chrysler take over the nose sections, but confident Bell executives cockily replied that "we are pretty well set up, and though we appreciate it, we don't need the help at this time." One officer said he was quite pleased with the progress made. "This is the first time that anybody has been pleased with anything to do with Bell's progress in the Georgia Division," noted a Bell writer.

Bell got a big boost when the Army Air Forces allowed Plant 6 to ignore ongoing design changes and modifications for its first twenty-five B-29s. It also approved Bell's reduced monthly output of forty aircraft to begin June 1944. In return, Bell agreed to start up a special modification center for its B-29s and for Wichita's, because, in the words of a Bell executive, "Wichita has limited space and we have plenty," thanks to Bell's reduced production quotas.

In the fall of 1943, Marietta B-29 planners ran up against another big problem that seemed to cancel the whole point of building Plant 6 in the first place—a serious shortage of workers. Many unemployed people lived in the area when planners selected Marietta.

During a shift change at Marietta. Workers pass through exits where guards check identities and for espionage and theft. Courtesy Atlanta History Center (BLL-3-17).

Teams of riveters on center wing sections at Bell–Marietta Plant 6. For every riveter, a bucker applied pressure on the other side. Courtesy Atlanta History Center (BLL-2-13).

But by the time the plant was ready to put large numbers of people to work, most had already found jobs.

Officials of the federal government's War Manpower Commission warned in September 1943 that "there are today substantially no unemployed persons in the Region," which included Georgia, the Carolinas, Florida, Alabama, and Tennessee. "The job of manning the Bell plant will not be easy." The problem, in a nutshell, was "to make people want to go to the Bell plant to work." But workers had plenty of reasons to not want to work there.

The most basic reason was the government's anti-inflation program and refusal to let aircraft companies across the country raise wages to levels that might have been competitive with other industries. In the South, aircraft wages—low as they were—still offered better incomes than most workers were used to during the Depression. But when Bell went looking for a large workforce beginning in the summer of 1943, these workers were doing much better or had been drafted. Farmers had found prosperity, the many great wartime construction projects in the South meant well-paying jobs, and, northwest of Atlanta, the old textile industry boomed because of huge wartime demand for the fabric that went into tires.

When planners chose the Marietta site, they expected that nearly 40,000 production workers would be needed. Since the population of Cobb County was 35,000, the great majority of Bell workers would have to come from surrounding counties. Planners hoped that many workers would come from Atlanta, 20 miles away. But few plans had been made for easing "the personal hardship and difficulty" of getting to and from Marietta every day, or of moving there. Cars and buses were scarce and only limited new housing was available near the plant.

At a time when many Americans believed that victory in the war was practically "in the bag," Plant 6 didn't seem to offer jobs with much of a future. People were also suspicious of Bell and the whole project at Marietta. All the construction and planning delays led many to think of the project as a huge "military boondoggle" that would contribute nothing to the war effort and probably disgrace the area. "I realize that fighting a war is expensive but we don't have to deliberately throw away money," complained a citizen of Acworth, Georgia, in November 1943 to Sen. Harry Truman, chairman of the Senate's "watchdog" committee on the defense industry. The size and expense of Plant 6 appalled him. "Not a single bomber has been produced." Bell was building a B-29 by hand, he wrote, "only to make a showing. . . . It's worse than any W.P.A. job."

And among the 8,000 or so already at work at Bell in the summer of 1943, "considerable underground muttering" could be heard about how Bell managers dealt with workers. Low pay and poor supervision made up the main complaints, and the new union, United Auto Workers Local 10, was in a weak position to do anything about them. In June 1943, 500 Bell workers quit.

Government officials decided that a major public relations effort had to be launched in an attempt to squelch rumors and attract workers. "We will have to marshal all of the forces of the community, together with the full impact of the Government and its publicity sources, toward getting recognition of the prime importance of this plant." One bulletin said that "the women of Atlanta, of all social strata, should prepare themselves and their affairs so that they may take their patriotic and useful part in making this plant a success—a success that may considerably hasten the end of the war."

It became obvious that the only real hope of manning the plant was to tap into and expand the "substantial labor resources in terms of women." Nearly 60 percent of the workforce would have to be made up by women even though planners realized that a "woman in her home, maintaining her family, cannot be regarded as unemployed." The publicity campaign, better transportation facilities—especially a new four-lane freeway from Atlanta to Marietta—more housing, day-care provisions, paid training programs, giant cafeterias, bonuses for the night shift, all made work at Marietta more attractive and led to a very rapid increase in the workforce in

Preparing a B-29 tail for
its rudder. Courtesy
Atlanta History Center
(BLL-3-0).

Workers do installations on nose sections out of their jigs. This scene couldn't be repeated today. These workers are breaking just about every one of today's safety rules for factory work. Courtesy Atlanta History Center (BLL-2-9).

late 1943 and early 1944. Officials of the federal War Manpower Commission and U.S. Employment Service took over most of Bell's responsibilities in hiring and labor relations. They took sophisticated approaches to the problem and worked out incentives that helped reshuffle workers among local war industries.

In November 1943 alone, Bell hired 3,379 women and men. By the end of 1944, 17,200 worked at Plant 6. Employment of both direct and indirect workers peaked at 27,000 in the spring of 1945. Of the workforce, 82 percent came from northwest Georgia, the rest from elsewhere.

Planners managed this impressive feat of gathering up workers despite the fact that few African-Americans were hired except for janitorial or other such work. As one official of the War Manpower Commission put it, hiring many blacks—"colored" workers—for responsible or even unskilled production jobs was too much for local "customs and habits" and the "peculiarities of temperament of Southern workers."

The great new workforce at Marietta only generated more complaints from local people as delays in actually turning out B-29s continued. Marietta now seemed massively overstaffed. Stories went around of how workers stood about "putting in time," "loafing," sleeping, and were made to "look busy" when inspectors and dignitaries showed up. The main causes of so much inactivity were poor supervision and the fact that tooling for B-29s was behind schedule. Bell's lofting system proceeded very slowly and engineers still needed basic information on the B-29. "We're 40 miles from nowhere on getting data," complained Larry Bell.

Most planners and officers blamed Bell's company, but he pointed out that "we aren't alone in this thing." Design changes especially "hurt like hell." Bell complained about "the awful beating . . . our meager organization" took, especially from critics at Boeing who worried about Bell and Marietta as a possible long-term competitor building large aircraft. Bell and his executives spent much of their energy defending the company's name. The Army Air Forces wanted to keep paring down Marietta's production schedule and shift scarce materials and supplies to the other plants—especially Wichita. But more schedule reductions would have been bad for the Bell name and Larry Bell stubbornly fought them. He even managed to squeeze out a $200-million contract for another 300 B-29s and promised more parts—mainly wing spars—for the other plants. Still, the B-29's problems and the scale of Marietta overwhelmed the company. Bell also was at work in Buffalo on a new attack plane, the P-63, and America's first jet plane, the XP-59.

Marietta's first B-29 rolled out in November 1943, taking to the air on the fourth. General Wolfe said the plant had "hacked out the first sample article." But he was pleased with the progress, telling Bell that "I really didn't think you could do it." More B-29s slowly rolled out of Plant 6 during the first half of 1944. The first fifteen were basically handmade with many outside parts. All spent long periods in modification. In July 1944, Charles E. Wilson, chairman of the Aircraft Production Board in Washington, D.C., expressed his "keen disappointment with Bell." And the AAF Office of Flying Safety criticized Marietta B-29s as "far below the standards required for aircraft used in combat."

Bell executives worried about what the B-29 might do to their careers and "the fact that it is possible that we may be unduly criticized by some one of the various investigating committees as to why this facility is not producing airplanes at the required rate." But the fact that Bell turned out any airplanes as complex as the B-29 is remarkable, especially in view of the workers' inexperience and the constant design changes. Despite all the problems, the first Marietta B-29 flew less than two years after workers broke ground for Plant 6. True production finally kicked in in the fall of 1944. Then Plant 6 began meeting, even exceeding, its much-reduced plans.

Public attitudes toward Bell and the Marietta project became much more positive. Local newswriters boasted that Bell built B-29s "cocked for battle." In truth, though, most Bell B-29s were "stripped ships" needing many modifications and installations after assembly and much of this work was done elsewhere. Not until June 1945 did workers manage to get more than half of the B-29's modifications into the assembly lines. Still, managers and 27,000 workers, on two daily nine-hour shifts, had turned B-29 production into such a steady routine that Bell executives agreed to convert their contracts to the fixed-price basis.

Executives had greatly reduced the cost of building Bell B-29s. In March 1945, the company agreed on 500 B-29s for only $240,000 apiece—about what a B-17 cost in 1940. Of course, Bell's charges only covered materials, wages, salaries, and the profit. They didn't include "government furnished equipment"—engines, landing gear, radar, and so on through a very long list. And they did not include "overhead"—especially the costs for the enormous plant and all its gear. So efficient had the plant become that in June 1945 the work week was cut to five days with weekends off. The change could be made even though the quit rate grew steadily as workers sensed the war might soon be over and B-29 production halted.

The people of Atlanta and Georgia now glowed about Plant 6 and the B-29. Newspapers featured many stories about both, as well as accounts of how the B-29s were being used in the war. "Georgia's Birds of Vengeance" was how one reporter tagged the Bell B-29s. "The birds of retribution, swift, sinister, silver, that would lay their eggs of death over Nippon were hatched on a Georgia hillside all in view of Kennesaw Mountain." One writer explained that the B-29s coming out of Marietta would "whale the daylights out of the enemy." Another hailed the "thunderstorms of bombs" over Japanese cities. Using a common racial slur, still another writer praised "the great silver dragons" that "will be pouring it on the Japs as payment of principal and interest for the outrage of Pearl Harbor."

Such lurid praise for the B-29 expressed the bitter feelings most Americans held for the Japanese. In the Atlanta area it also served to heighten a sense of achievement at Marietta after so many delays and frustrations and at a time when postwar military spending at the plant was much in doubt. The local media boosted Larry Bell and his executives into Georgian heroes in 1945. So strong was public feeling for Marietta that the role of James V. Carmichael, a Cobb County native, as general manager at Bell helped him win the popular vote for governor in the 1946 election. He was defeated, however, by Eugene Talmadge's Democratic machine in Georgia's version of the electoral college.

The outpouring of local praise for the B-29 and Bell–Marietta, especially from Atlanta businessmen, newspapers, and boosters, was also a reflex animated by anxiety over what the true story of Marietta might do for their visions and dreams of a New South—a South of advanced industries, better lifestyles, economic growth, and "free enterprise." In the end, however, the limits of Marietta's B-29 program, especially compared to Wichita and Omaha, did not stand in the way. Employment was slashed in the late summer of 1945 and the plant closed in 1946, a significant blow to the economy of northwestern Georgia.

Plant 6 served for four years, however, as a huge Air Force warehouse and transfer station where the government auctioned off to private businessmen mountains of machine tools and industrial gear at fire-sale prices, equipment that had cost the taxpayer hundreds of millions of dollars. Then under a lease, Lockheed reopened Plant 6, putting thousands of Southerners back to work as builders of very large military aircraft. It remains a pillar of the New South into the 1990s.

WHO BUILT THE ENGINES?

The B-29's success depended not just on developing and producing the airframe, but also on a range of other products and technologies. The B-29 needed engines, propellers, and landing gear, as well as systems for navigation, communication, cabin pressurization, engine supercharging, defensive guns, and so on. These were developed by such companies as Bendix, General Electric, Sperry, Burroughs, Hamilton-Standard, Curtiss-Wright, A. O. Smith, and Honeywell. Like the planners setting up the national network for mass-producing the B-29 airframe, these companies began their work in concurrence with the XB-29's development, long before anyone knew if these products and systems would work. One nervous planner accurately warned that it all "depends upon everything clicking as planned."

Of all the systems the B-29 relied on, none was more crucial than its engines. And none posed more of a threat to the project's success. Whether its giant R-3350 Cyclone engines would work reliably and whether they could be mass-produced in large numbers were big questions that hung over the B-29 program well into 1944.

An enormous aircooled duplex-piston engine, the R-3350 had eighteen cylinders packed around the crankshaft core. Two radial rings of nine cylinders displaced a total of 3,350 cubic inches. Like two wheels on a hub, the cylinder heads reached outward for cooling by the wind pushed around them by the big props. Seventy-six inches long, the R-3350 could run at 2,000 horsepower for cruising and 2,200 for takeoff. It would be twice as powerful as the B-17's engine, but have the same air resistance—a frontal exposure of only 55 inches around. That meant that an engine twice the size of the B-17 engine had to be cooled by the same airflow.

The problem with the R-3350 design was not that it was so advanced but how it stretched the limits of air-cooled engine design. The R-3350 had been worked on since 1935 by engineers at Wright Aeronautical, a Curtiss-Wright company in Paterson, New Jersey. Along with Pratt & Whitney of Hartford, Connecticut, Wright was one of the only two large aircraft–engine manufacturers in the United States. Still, as late as the attack on Pearl Harbor, the R-3350 wasn't much more than an experiment—much like the XB-29.

Engineers hoped the R-3350 would be the ideal aircraft engine—"one pound of weight for every horsepower produced." It would be as powerful as the average railroad locomotive but would weigh

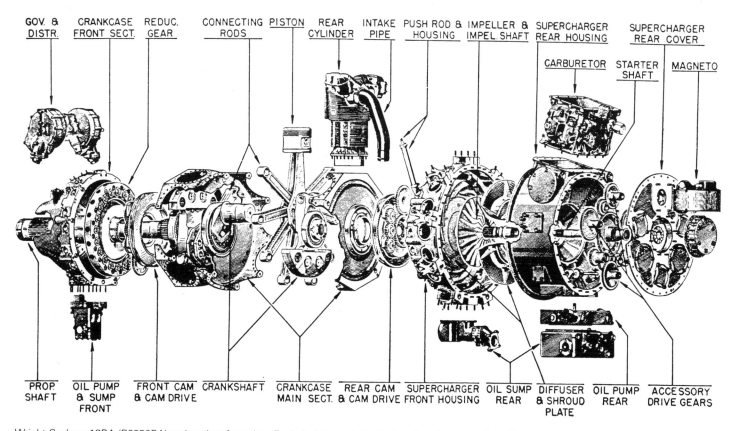

GOV. & DISTR.   CRANKCASE FRONT SECT.   REDUC. GEAR   CONNECTING RODS   PISTON   REAR CYLINDER   INTAKE PIPE   PUSH ROD & HOUSING   IMPELLER & IMPEL. SHAFT   SUPERCHARGER REAR HOUSING   SUPERCHARGER REAR COVER

CARBURETOR   STARTER SHAFT   MAGNETO

PROP SHAFT   OIL PUMP & SUMP FRONT   FRONT CAM & CAM DRIVE   CRANKSHAFT   CRANKCASE MAIN SECT.   REAR CAM & CAM DRIVE   SUPERCHARGER FRONT HOUSING   OIL SUMP REAR   DIFFUSER & SHROUD PLATE   OIL PUMP REAR   ACCESSORY DRIVE GEARS

Wright Cyclone 18BA (R3350BA) series aircraft engine: Exploded view of a typical engine. Courtesy of the National Air and Space Museum, Smithsonian Institution, Peece Collection.

only as much as the locomotive's wheels. Although the basic technology of the big air-cooled engines had been mastered in the 1920s, the R-3350 was very ambitious. Planners expected most of the complicated problems that came up. But since the R-3350 would power the B-29, the time it took to solve these problems frustrated those working on the engine. Relations between the Army and the Wright company were often so bad that the company would threaten to bail out and leave the government with nothing to show for its huge investment.

Wright began testing the first R-3350 in 1937. It had run for 135 hours on the test stand when its reduction gears began to fail—a problem not really solved until 1943. In 1939, two other basic problems appeared—failures in the exhaust valve and cooling systems—which engineers never really straightened out at all.

WHO BUILT THE ENGINES?

The development process was slowed in the R-3350's early years because so few financial incentives existed for aircraft and engine designers under the Army's old contracting rules. Those rules made the aircraft engine business as unprofitable and risky as the airframe business, which made Boeing's early development of the XB-29 so difficult. Almost every costly innovation and new step the Wright company took was at its own financial risk. And the company's Curtiss-Wright parent was not profitable in the 1930s. But when Congress changed the rules in 1940 to make it easier for the Army and Navy and engine companies to develop new aircraft products, Wright executives and managers found themselves snowed under with wartime orders for their already proven engines like the R-1820, which powered the B-17. They had trouble finding engineers and managers for the R-3350.

Wright didn't commit a large number of engineers until early 1942. Company executives didn't push the design as aggressively as they might have or wanted to. Also, they proved themselves not really up to running the company, which as part of its Curtiss-Wright parent company suddenly ballooned from an employer of a few hundred workers into a giant defense contractor with hundreds of thousands of employees in many states.

The R-3350 program succeeded, however, in spite of all the delays and technical problems. The Army Air Forces mounted a vigorous effort to solve the problems and to clear its production bottlenecks, which all came to a head in the fall of 1943. And engineers managed to squeeze out a war rating of nearly 2,600 horsepower from the engine by 1944. They also made it more reliable. In 1944, workers built R-3350s at the staggering rate of 11,000 per year even though the engine needed constant engineering changes.

Wright Aeronautical, still a long way from producing a reliable R-3350, received its first production order for the engine in May 1941. The Army ordered 185 for the XB-29s, YB-29s, and some other new aircraft designs, but only one production engine was available by December 1941. In the summer of 1942, the company began tooling up for the R-3350 in a huge new plant going up at Woodridge, New Jersey, not far from the present Meadowlands Sports Complex near New York City. The taxpayer covered the cost of the land, buildings, foundries, and equipment for this 1.5 million square–foot complex.

Government planners who chose the site worried about air attacks and the "exposed location" of Woodridge to the sea. "It will be difficult to justify the location of a new airplane engine plant of large capacity at a place so close to the coast," especially since Wright and Pratt & Whitney already seemed in danger at their locations near New York City. Some argued that St. Louis, Milwaukee, Minneapolis, or Birmingham, Alabama, was a safer choice.

Top Army and War Department leaders finally chose the Woodridge site. Undersecretary of War Robert Patterson, Chief of Staff Gen. George Marshall, and Assistant Secretary of War for Air Robert Lovett reasoned that "the large and experienced industrial labor pool around New York City" and the availability of electric power to run the plant's machines and foundries offset "the factor of hostile bombing." By the end of 1944, planners spent nearly $70 million on Woodridge's plant and equipment alone.

But Wright–Woodridge had its problems, mainly, as it turned out, shortages of trained personnel. And it proved wasteful setting up foundries, metal-cutting equipment and tooling for a product as complicated as the R-3350 when so many basic changes were still being made in the design. The government agency that oversaw allocations of machine tools and key metals to all defense contractors realized this early on and gave Wright's R-3350 program a low priority.

But War Department officials trying to move the very heavy bomber program along fought for the engine. The R-3350 and the B-29 got big boosts after Pearl Harbor, especially in January 1942 when the Chrysler Corporation agreed to mass-produce the engine. There seemed no room for restraint in the first weeks of U.S. involvement in the war. Officials promised Chrysler a 6 percent cost-plus-fixed-fee contract worth $313 million to build 10,000 R-

3350s plus spare parts. In March, the contract grew to 17,653 R-3350s worth $594 million. Through its Dodge division, Chrysler would build and operate a massive new complex of factories on a 450-acre site at 7401 South Cicero Street on Chicago's West Side.

At the peak of activity, about 20,000 construction people worked on the nineteen Dodge–Chicago buildings, which covered 6.3 million square feet. It was the largest manufacturing facility in the world. Plant 4, the assembly and machine shop building, was the biggest single factory anywhere, measuring nearly 4 million square feet. Dodge–Chicago had the world's biggest parking lot and its 9,300 new metal-cutting machines made up the biggest order for such equipment ever made.

By 1944, the government had committed more than three-quarters of a billion dollars to Dodge–Chicago. Land and the plant's construction and equipment cost $175 million. These costs, like those on the B-29 plants and equipment, were not computed into the actual costs of engine production. Once the plant was up and running, it cost about $25,000 for each R-3350. That figure included only materials and wages and the big contracts let to Wright and Dodge only reflected those cost factors.

Chrysler said it would start delivery in March 1943. But the operating manager at Dodge–Chicago felt obliged to explain in the summer of 1942 that "we have had all kinds of difficulties trying to get started." Deals with real estate agents, architects, and builders took much longer than expected and construction didn't begin until June. The company also had the usual trouble getting blueprints, parts lists, and other data on the engine from Wright, a hardly surprising situation since the R-3350 was still under development. Also, during these months severe national shortages of steel, aluminum, and magnesium caused bottlenecks. The federal agency overseeing aluminum and magnesium stocks put Dodge–Chicago low on the priority list. Chrysler insisted its first delivery date be pushed back to July 1943.

Wright managed to produce only about twenty-five unreliable R-3350s by the time the XB-29 first flew in late September 1942.

Piston ring, reduction gear, and cooling failures were the main culprits. With no immediate solutions in sight it seemed that all the effort and money put into the B-29 program might be wasted. One top staff general bitterly wrote:

> Trying to find out just what active steps are being taken to correct the 3350 situation, i.e. "Who is doing what and where are they going to get it done?" has been like trying to gather a handful of cobwebs. . . . Many just around the corner solutions are being put forward but we have now reached that corner and are in serious trouble.

He criticized Wright executives and engineers for "always having plenty of alibis" and AAF officers for being "wishy-washy" and pursuing a "hands-off policy" in their dealings with Wright.

It seemed that no one wanted responsibility for making decisions in the R-3350 program. The stakes were high. Making bad decisions in a project with so much money committed might permanently damage professional careers in the Army and aircraft industry. And Curtiss-Wright, the holding company that controlled the engine, was too old-fashioned and stubborn in matters of management. The company had exploded in size with giant new aircraft, engine, and propeller branch plants in New Jersey, New York, Pennsylvania, Ohio, Indiana, Missouri, and Kentucky. Wright was the largest producer of aircraft engines in the United States. In 1939 it had 10,000 employees, but in 1943 more than 140,000 and growing fast. Indeed, in contract size, Curtiss-Wright was the second largest military contractor in the United States after General Motors.

The company quickly became a giant firm manufacturing very complex equipment. Yet its top executives refused or didn't know how to delegate authority and allow managers in its various divisions to use their own initiative. Everything important had to be cleared through Curtiss-Wright headquarters in the skyscrapers of Rockefeller Plaza in New York City. Members of the Aircraft

Production Board in Washington, D.C., complained that the "Curtiss-Wright policy of non-resident management is undesirable." But its top executives "will not agree to decentralization."

Led by Guy W. Vaughan, chairman of the board, top officers and investors at Curtiss-Wright worried about losing control of a company whose huge new wartime size seemed only temporary and whose future at war's end was anybody's guess. They worried about criticism, even criminal action, if things went seriously wrong with all that taxpayer money invested. As one Wright executive put it, "I don't want to have to appear before any Truman group," referring to Sen. Harry Truman's high-profile watchdog committee in Congress. The company found it hard to attract good executives who could run a plant like Woodridge because most thought of Curtiss-Wright as a "war job" with a risky future.

The government never forced the Curtiss-Wright people to change. It never took over the company even though it figured so crucially in the war effort, stumbled badly in its work, and made top people in the government very angry. Curtiss-Wright's relation with the government is another important example of how federal policymakers and planners avoided the government's heavy hand as much as they possibly could during the war. Most of these advisors were themselves temporary recruits from big business who didn't want to give up too much on the limited way the government regulates business in America and wanted to preserve, as much as they could, traditional American values of private enterprise, the individual, and voluntarism.

Fortunately for Americans and their political traditions, the real fighting war took place far away across the oceans, something they experienced mainly through the media. The "war emergency" always seemed a bit abstract. And the U.S. economy was so big, had so many natural resources, raw materials, and people to do the work, that World War II's urgency never seemed to call for aggressive government solutions. Thus companies like Curtiss-Wright had room to make mistakes and had whatever time or luck they needed to straighten things out. America's enemies had none of these luxuries. As one insightful worker at the B-29 modification center in Birmingham put it in 1943, "This country seems to be able to do more by accident than any other country can do on purpose."

The R-3350's technical and production problems were slowly ironed out, but they hobbled the B-29 program through 1943 and 1944. In February 1943, General Arnold ordered all R-3350s grounded after engine fires caused one of the XB-29s to crash in Seattle. Its crew members were killed, including Eddie Allen, Boeing's famous test pilot, along with thirty-one people on the ground. Arnold boiled with anger as he contemplated the R-3350 situation. He ordered a new special board to study and test the engine.

That board soon assured him of the R-3350's progress and predicted that the engine would eventually be reliable and could be mass-produced. But the board warned that it needed basic engineering changes, greater attention from AAF officers, and higher priorities for raw materials and machine tools. Until then, severe production problems would continue at Wright–Woodridge and Dodge–Chicago. Machine tools and mass-production lines couldn't be set up until the design had been finalized.

From January to November 1943 alone, engineers made some 2,000 changes, 500 of which required tooling changes. This meant that technicians and highly skilled workers basically made R-3350s by hand, on "pilot lines"—assembly lines kept flexible enough so that the endless changes could be easily included. The theory was that once the engine was finalized, mass-production lines would be built based on the pilot line's model.

In the summer of 1943, only the pilot line at Wright Plant 7 in Woodridge operated at all. Dodge–Chicago wasn't nearly ready. Yet, planners felt cause for hope. In July 1943, technicians tested the first engine with the changes recommended by the special board with good results. They hoped the changes could be squeezed into pilot lines by November 1943, which would mean large numbers of "combat engines."

The Greenlea Multiple Machine, the most impressive of Wright's automated factory equipment. Stretching 154 feet, the Greenlea Machine automatically performed eighty different operations on R-3350 cylinder heads. Courtesy of the National Air and Space Museum, Smithsonian Institution, Peece Collection.

But through the summer and fall of 1943, delay after delay rocked the R-3350 program. Production B-29s came off the line at last in Wichita, but there weren't enough engines for them, or to keep the B-29's flying through the long training programs for B-29 crews. Rumors spread in the media and in Congress about how badly the project had fallen behind, forcing an angry General Arnold to give the R-3350 and B-29 programs his personal attention once again. He now called the R-3350 "the Number 1 requirement of the Army Air Forces."

On Arnold's orders, AAF officers launched new investigations and began taking aggressive steps to get the R-3350 program moving. One group of investigators sent to Wright–Woodridge included the young James McDonnell, founder of McDonnell Aircraft, Lt. Col. William J. Brennan Jr., the future Supreme Court Justice, and William O'Dwyer, the district attorney who became mayor of New York. These men found little wrongdoing, but plenty of incompetence and apathy on management's part as well as big shortages of workers.

At a time when Woodridge Plant 7 was supposed to have over 8,000 direct production workers, it only had 3,300. Wright couldn't train or attract enough workers to its plant and could barely hold on to the ones it had. Its problems were similar to those faced at the same time by Boeing in Seattle, Bell in Atlanta, and many other aircraft companies.

Wright's reputation as an employer in the New York City area was very bad. In 1931, it broke a machinists' union after a long, bitter, and violent strike. And through the 1930s it used all kinds of tactics—legal and illegal—to keep wages low and to make sure that real collective bargaining did not develop. Wright had to fight unions because it couldn't be profitable under Congress's rules for military aircraft sales. And again, during the war years, the federal government worked to keep wages in aircraft down as part of its attempt to control inflation.

One Army inspector summed up the results at Wright–Woodridge

in mid-1943: "Due to the low starting wages paid by this corporation, it has become common practice for new personnel to take advantage of the training and then leave the employ of Wright Aeronautical for better paying positions." In July, the company hired 2,340 people. But 1,762 quit—1,304 for better jobs and 458 because the military draft took them. "From the public relations point of view, the company stands very low in the estimation of the local public." Among those who stayed at Wright, daily absenteeism was "7 per cent and rising."

Planners started Plant 7 hoping that workers from the Bronx, Brooklyn, Queens, Long Island, and Newark could be drawn there. But if the starting wage of 60 cents an hour wasn't bad enough, the long commute across the New Jersey Meadowlands settled the issue for many of the best workers. In those days, the return trip took 4½ hours. Workers naturally preferred better paying, closer jobs in the many other local defense industries, especially the shipyards.

As a result, some of the most inexperienced workers in the region worked on the R-3350, the most complicated single product then being mass-produced in the United States. Production at the plant soon fell well below schedule and was basically out of control. Giant machines milled out parts that weren't being assembled. Piles of wasted material started to build as workers made many mistakes. "In the crankcase and major housing departments, three members of Inspection Supervision have been so affected . . . that they are currently seeking psychiatric treatment," read one government report in the late summer of 1943.

The problem was mainly one of supervision. Despite the R-3350's complexity, factory planners so thoroughly broke down and mechanized the production and assembly process that the large majority of workers could be unskilled or semi-skilled. Building aircraft engines had always required the closest attention from highly skilled machinists and mechanics who carefully cut, honed, bored, and ground aluminum, magnesium, and steel parts by hand or on a

The original caption on this photo read: "The final inspection of finished R-3350 crankcases is safely entrusted to the dexterous fingers of women inspectors. A complete set of foolproof gauges assures one hundred percent inspection." Courtesy of the National Air and Space Museum, Smithsonian Institution, Peece Collection.

wide range of machinery to make cylinder barrels, crankshafts, pistons, rocker arms, and so on until the engine was ready. Engines required the most careful and finest work. There was no room for error. Parts had to fit perfectly.

But with the huge wartime demand for aircraft engines, specially designed machines took over the cutting, milling, and honing of parts that made up most of the production process. The main job for aircraft engine workers became tending the same machines and equipment, hour after hour, day in, day out. The other major group of jobs in the plant—assembly, inspection, and testing—had also been broken up so new workers could easily handle them. The factory system had been put in place and most of the work was simple. But Wright managers weren't showing people how to do it. Officers complained of poor supervision and low morale among Plant 7 workers, who often had nothing to do.

Many used their idle time standing around, sleeping, or playing poker and craps. Their jobs seemed useless, the pay was bad, and their new union—the United Automobile Workers of America—paid little attention to them. "Plant 7 is living a hand to mouth existence," warned one officer. "Loitering and gambling are common with large groups concentrated in the toilets for long periods."

The situation only began turning around in September 1943 when the War Department sent experts to show Wright managers how to run the plant and deal with its labor problems. With the help of the War Manpower Commission, the federal agency that oversaw the nation's war labor supply, they rearranged the work process. They also changed the company's hiring approach, insisting that unskilled women and African-Americans could do the work and that the company drop its prejudices against them.

They improved training for new workers and set up a Knowledge of the Product program. Before, supervisors had taken a "work and don't ask questions" attitude. Now, workers had tours of the far-flung plant so they could get a sense of their roles in the larger picture. Workers also sat through detailed discussions of the military plans for the R-3350 and B-29, how the engine ran, and the importance of each part and each worker's job in turning it out.

Government officials and the company launched an advertising campaign in New York City to impress workers with Plant 7's special importance and the fact that its engines powered the new "superbombers." Subsidized buses now ran to and from Manhattan. "Child nurseries," bank facilities, stores, and cafeterias appeared. And the Muzak Company installed piped-in tunes to attract new workers to Plant 7 and keep them building R-3350s.

The company transferred 300 skilled workers from its other plants and the Army Air Forces moved men from its airbase maintenance shops to train new workers. Wright executives agreed to use areas in its new branch plants in Lockland, Ohio, near Cincinnati, and in East Paterson and Fairlawn, New Jersey, to make R-3350 parts. These plants were financed and built by the government. At Lockland alone, it cost $20 million to convert for the R-3350.

Planners arranged an integrated parts program between Wright and Dodge–Chicago, allowing each plant to specialize on parts they exchanged with one another to speed output. And planners found new subcontractors: American Radiator of Elyria, Ohio; Studebaker of South Bend, Indiana; U.S. Radiator of Geneva, New York; Bohn Aluminum of Detroit, and Dow Chemical of Bay City, Michigan. Chrysler put many of its workers in Detroit and in Kokomo and New Castle, Indiana, to work on R-3350 parts.

At Woodridge, morale among the workers improved. One women from the Bronx felt glad about working for the "battle effort." "We've all got to stick to our jobs to get these engines out so we can get those B-29s across the water where they can knock hell out of the Japs." A 20-year-old woman from Georgia, working an air-wrench on the R-3350's rocker arms, said, "Well . . . I had a boyfriend in the Air Forces. He was killed four months ago. I decided I wanted to do something besides farm and I thought if I could help to build airplanes that would be the best way to prevent lots of other boys from being killed the way my friend was."

Women made the difference at Woodridge. One foreman said that "generally the women are more conscientious and energetic workers. . . . They are the ones who will complain when there is a lack of work and who will dig in and get a job finished when there is work at hand. On the other hand, the average male worker will try to stretch the job."

The key to movement on the R-3350 program was General Arnold's work at the high levels of bureaucracy and politics in Washington, D.C. He and his assistants lobbied for a special wage increase at Woodridge. They wanted 85 cents per hour for the starting wage and insisted that the National War Labor Board "get off its ass on this." But they had to settle for 70 cents, gradual raises with time on the job, and a new bonus system tying workers' pay to the amount they produced. Minimum pay went to 85 cents in the foundries, where the work with molten metal was hot, heavy, and dirty.

By the end of October, employment at Plant 7 surged. The company hired 1,000 new workers in that month alone, bringing the total to 9,700, well on the way to the goal of 13,200. By late November 1943, officers predicted the plant would turn out 800 engines per month beginning in January 1944. Satisfied with their work, they left Plant 7, and allowed Wright executives to operate it alone from that point on.

At Dodge–Chicago, the fall of 1943 was also a time of frustrating delays for the R-3350 and the B-29 program. Some 20,000 construction workers finished the giant factory complex in April 1943, but shortages of machines, constant engineering changes, and communication problems on technical matters with the Wright company in New Jersey prevented full operation of even the pilot line. Chrysler executives promised "we will do everything we can." But in November 1943, the two main production lines still needed almost 300 major machine tools. Complete engines weren't produced at Dodge–Chicago until January 1944. By that point, though, the worst design bugs had been worked out of the R-3350 and the plant tooled and staffed.

One officer was happy to report to General Arnold that "Dodge now seems to be on the beam." Another said that "components flow is good and final assembly is well under way, although the line is by no means filled." Once the big engines started coming, they came in streams. By war's end, workers at Dodge–Chicago built 18,500 R-3350s.

On average, about 33,000 people worked at Dodge–Chicago in 1944 and the first half of 1945. Direct production workers made up 16,000 of these—8,800 on the day shift, 6,600 on the night shift, and 600 on maintenance and cleanup in the morning shift. Another 17,000 white-collars did the purchasing, accounting, engineering, and other paperwork. Women made up 35 percent of the workforce and African-Americans about 20 percent. In the hot, heavy work at the foundry, half of the workers were black.

Mass production of the R-3350 during 1943–45 is striking on so many levels—the scale of the factories and machinery; the size and inexperience of the workforce; the power and complexity of the engine; the endless supplies of raw materials and parts; and the vast numbers of engines turned out. What is most striking, though, is how unorganized the production process was, how there was no obvious "system."

At Dodge–Chicago, inspectors from the War Manpower Commission who tried to figure out how this giant factory was organized found no formal structure of job descriptions or duties in the spring of 1945. The company "hired the gate," which meant whoever applied got a job. Men and women were given basic instructions and went to work. Commission experts marveled at how people used their own initiative to complete their jobs and then found ways to help others and make themselves useful. Executives, supervisors, inspectors, foremen, skilled and unskilled production workers formed teams. They ran up against problems on the factory floor together and then dealt with them.

There were no organization charts, flow charts, or clear systems of command and control. People made decisions and gave instructions to each other. Commission experts described these word-of-mouth relations as "oral and conference methods of communication," and "oral understanding and instruction." Few memos were sent with orders handed down from above. In the vast Dodge–Chicago complex, only one old copy of Management Fundamentals could be found by the inspectors. And only five AAF officers were posted in the whole complex.

Mass production of the R-3350 engine was the work of teams, even if tens of thousands of people were involved. The production system was set up quickly and in accord with the rule of "making do." Experts in manufacturing systems complained about how unstructured the engine plants were and their big demands in a very tight labor market. They accused Chrysler of thinking, "Well, anything goes on cost-plus contracts." But it was hard to argue with success—the thousands of B-29 powerplants turned out along an ever-rising efficiency curve.

By late 1944, workers at Dodge–Chicago regularly exceeded production schedules. In November 1944, they built 1,079 engines and thousands of critical parts for the Woodridge and Lockland plants. Costs per engine went down to $15,080 each in 1945. That figure, again, did not include overhead or capital investment—more than $100 million in taxpayer money that went into building the plant and tooling it up.

Penalty engines—new R-3350s that didn't survive their hours of running in the test cells—were reduced from 31 percent of total production in the spring of 1944 to 2 percent in the spring of 1945. And, incredibly, technicians discovered in May 1944 that "the engine parts manufactured by the Dodge–Chicago plant were found to be completely interchangeable in engines made by the Wright Aeronautical Corporation."

Still, getting up to R-3350 mass production was never smooth sailing. In the spring and summer of 1944 especially, workers at Woodridge couldn't meet their schedules mainly because of the company's trouble finding good people to supervise. Gen. William Knudsen, who had been president of General Motors but worked for the Army during the war, summed up Plant 7's problems in mid-1944 as a "general lack of organization or interest on the part of management and top supervisory personnel . . . bad planning, bad supervision . . . rate of rework runs at 50–60 percent . . . a very high scrap heap."

At both Woodridge and Dodge–Chicago "individual bottlenecks" interfered with R-3350 output in 1944—breakdowns in machinery and shortages of key materials and parts, especially crankshafts and reduction gears. And turnover remained a big problem, even though many more engines could be built by fewer and fewer workers as the learning curve went up. People quit their "war job" when an opportunity came with a future beyond V-J day. The quit rate rose especially after D day and again in the months of spring 1945. Labor turnover rates in the B-29 program as a whole mean that total employment figures must be raised by about 60 percent to get a true sense of the number of Americans who built the B-29.

Dodge–Chicago workers overcame such problems, but R-3350 production through 1944–45 was still always limited by how the engine itself needed constant modifications. For example, to get more horsepower to carry the B-29's ever-growing weight designers replaced the R-3350's carburetors with a complicated fuel injection system developed by the Bosch Company. But finding ways to improve the engine's cooling caused the main difficulties for engineers.

Of all the B-29's systems, engine cooling posed the biggest challenges for pilots, crews, and maintenance people. Many B-29s were lost to engine overheating and fires. "There are innumerable mechanical difficulties and continual repairs and adjustments are required to keep the power plant systems in safe working order," reported one B-29 maintenance officer. In the first half of 1944, fires started seven out of ten times a B-29 had engine failure in flight.

Workers warm up an R-3350 at Boeing Field in Seattle, with a fire extinguisher always at the ready. Courtesy of the Boeing Company (X16).

The virtual "certainty of fire" led many crews to bail out quickly in times of engine trouble, leaving the aircraft to come crashing down. Who could blame them with the big fuel tanks in the B-29's wings? As late as January 1945, the commander of B-29 training in Colorado Springs complained that "I am still having fires." By that point, though, the sheer numbers of R-3350s turned out at Woodridge and Chicago overwhelmed these problems.

Dodge–Chicago helped make up production shortfalls at Woodridge in the spring and early summer of 1944. Meanwhile, the problems at Plant 7 were smoothed out. By the fall of 1944, workers turned out so many engines that they exceeded demand for the B-29s and for the other aircraft using the R-3350: the Martin Mars flying boat, the Douglas BTD Skyraider carrier attack plane, and Lockheed's new airliner, the Constellation.

Indeed, by August 1944, planners called for a scaling back of R-3350 production and tried to figure out how to store the excess engines. Maintenance officers found it easier and cheaper to replace a worn out R-3350 with a factory-fresh one and junk the old rather than overhaul it. Workers built so many of them that the mighty R-3350 had became a disposable engine.

CONCLUSION

Americans have built many other bombers since the B-29, all of them far more complex and powerful than the Superfortress. But none were design developed, and mass-produced so quickly and with such urgency. None involved so much new planning and organization in so short a time or posed so many challenges to the usual patterns of American social life.

Building the B-29 was actually a series of success stories. The Superfortress needed many different new technologies and production processes. Designing and building the airframe and engines posed their own separate problems—all luckily solved at about the same time. The B-29's avionics and computerized guns were other problems that threatened the whole program. Planners, designers, and workers solved those problems, too.

Finding solutions and timing them so that the B-29 program's various parts clicked was never a sure thing. The success suggests the power and depth of the American economy and the unique way Americans organized themselves for achieving national goals. Would the government have to force people to work the way it

drafted soldiers to fight? Or would New York City and eastern New Jersey provide enough motivated workers to build the R-3350 at Woodridge? Would men and women in Chicago be drawn to the great Dodge plant? Would a very complicated life in Seattle still make a work-a-day-week on B-29s an option for people there? Would Georgians see their opportunities somewhere other than in Marietta? How much of the program rode on the unique abilities and willing-to-work attitudes in Omaha and Wichita?

Americans built nearly 4,000 B-29s plus their spare parts. Plans were in the works to build another 2,000 when the war suddenly ended. These 2,000 would have been much cheaper because the manufacturing system was set up and in high gear. But the vast B-29 program was shut down almost overnight and practically all workers involved laid off.

The B-29's immediate effects on Americans were temporary and brief, but the long-term effects were deep and widespread. Workers, executives, and officers gained a range of industrial and planning skills that they used for a lifetime and taught to others along the way. The program showed the aircraft industry how to be both innovative and flexible enough to continue building the world's largest and most advanced aircraft. Indeed, the B-29 program taught the aircraft industry and the military much of what they know about producing complicated airplanes.

Working Americans designed and built the B-29. They also paid for it. The government created money to finance the war and big projects like the B-29. It then borrowed that money from people who could afford to buy the government's bonds. The principal and interest on these bonds were covered mainly by working Americans, who in 1943, for the first time, had income tax deducted from their paychecks. Through World War II programs such as the B-29, Americans were also introduced to the Pentagon's massive spending role, which continues to stimulate and shape the development of the U.S. economy.

About $3 billion was spent on nearly 4,000 B-29s plus spare parts. But the full cost of bombing Japan with B-29s is much greater. The $3-billion figure doesn't include the B-29's very expensive operational costs—base and runway construction; mainte-nance; crew training and pay; fuel, bombs, and many other supplies. And of course the development of the A-bomb cost another $2.5 billion.

These were huge sums of money for the time, nearly the largest amount ever spent for a single purpose. In 1990 dollars the B-29 cost roughly $30 billion. But just computing inflation into the figure doesn't give a true sense of the scope of the program because the size of the American economy and the number of Americans were much smaller during World War II than today.

To take a 1945 military accountant's view of "total war," the B-29 program against Japan paid off brutally but handsomely. Taking the costs of bombing Japan with B-29s as a whole and comparing them with an estimate of the total damage they caused produces the following: To drop one ton of bombs on Japan required 3.4 years of work by one American man or woman. To undo the damage of one ton of bombs, a man or woman in Japan would have to work for 50 years.

NOTE ON SOURCES

The information and all passages in quotation marks presented here are taken from original documents written during the late 1930s and during the 1940s. The most important source for research on B-29 development and production is the records of the Army Air Forces in the National Archives in Washington, D.C. Other AAF records on the B-29 can be found at the Simpson Research Center at Maxwell Air Force Base in Montgomery, Alabama, and at the Federal Records Center in St. Louis, Missouri.

Also important are records of civilian wartime agencies in the National Archives such as the Defense Plant Corporation, the War Manpower Commission, the National War Labor Board, the War Production Board, the Office of War Mobilization and Reconversion, the Office of War Information, and Sen. Harry Truman's special committee. There is also material at the regional branch of the National Archives in Atlanta.

The archives of the Boeing Corporation offered mainly a source of photographs. The records of the Aerospace Industries Association in the National Air and Space Museum give a good sense of the B-29 program's overall patterns and the problems of the aircraft industry as a whole. The museum also has a good collection of technical data and old photographs and movies. See especially the War Department films *B-29s over Dixie* and *The Birth of the B-29.*

Local newspapers—the *Wichita Eagle*, the *Omaha World-Herald*, the *Atlanta Constitution* and *Atlanta Journal*, the *Seattle Post-Intelligencer*, and the *New York Times*—are key to the B-29's social history. Other local sources on workers can be found at the Sarpy County Museum in Bellevue, Nebraska, the Chicago Historical Board, the Walter Reuther Library in Detroit, the public libraries in Omaha, Wichita, Seattle, Marietta, and Atlanta, the James Carmichael Collection at the Atlanta History Center, and the Library of Congress in Washington, D.C.

No single collection of documents on the B-29 program exists despite its importance to America's social, economic, and military history. This book was pieced together from original material scattered among all the sources listed above. To provide complete citations for these sources would require many pages of footnotes. Instead, a sampling of how these sources were used is offered below.

For the origins of the B-29 and on the development of the XB-29 see Tom Collison, *The Superfortress Is Born: The Story of the Boeing B-29* (New York, 1945), the only published study of the B-29's technical and production sides. Prof. Kenneth P. Werrell has a detailed and well-researched account in progress. See also W. F. Craven and J. L. Cate, *The Army Air Forces in World War II*, vol. 6, *Men and Planes* (Chicago, 1951), John A. Miller, *Men and Volts at War* (New York, 1947), and I. B. Holley Jr., *Buying Aircraft: Materiel Procurement for the Army Air Forces* (Washington, D.C., 1964).

I. B. Holley Jr. also wrote an important unpublished overview while the B-29 program was in full swing. See his declassified "The B-29," Historical Study No. 192 (April 21, 1945) at the Simpson Center at Maxwell Air Force Base. For negotiations between the Air Corps and the aircraft companies on a new long-range bomber, see Box 9, 452.1, Classified, and boxes 738, 740, 743, 747, 452.1, Unclassified, Series I, Records of the Army Adjutant General (AAG), 1939–42, Record Group 18, National Archives, Washington D.C. For the assessment of Boeing's XB-29 program by James Leland Atwood of North American Aviation, see Gen. Oliver P. Echols to Gen. George C. Kenney, October 22, 1941, Box 11, 452.1, Classified, AAG 39-42. For Col. L. F. Harman's comments on the XB-29 ("You can fly it quite easily"), see the transcript of his telephone conversation on October 1, 1942, with Gen. Oliver P. Echols in Box 110, 06-15-04-7-3, Federal Records Center, St. Louis, Missouri.

On the ideas and practice of strategic bombing see Michael Sherry, *The Rise of American Airpower* (New Haven, Conn., 1987); David MacIsaac, *Strategic Bombing in World War II* (New York, 1976); Henry H. Arnold, *Global Mission* (New York, 1949); and Ronald Schaffer, *Wings of Judgement: American Bombing in World War II* (New York, 1985). See also the ambitious scheme of Gen. K. B. Wolfe and L. F. Harman, "A Plan for the Employment of the B-29 Airplane against Japan Proper," April 18 1943, Box 691, 452.1, Bulky, Classified, AAG 1942–44.

Important accounts of the politics and problems of war mobilization include Eliot Janeway, *Struggle for Survival: A Chronicle of Economic Mobilization in World War II* (New Haven, 1951); R. E. Smith, *The Army and Economic Mobilization* (Washington, 1959); Harold Vatter, *The U.S. Economy in World War II* (New York, 1985); Bruce Catton, *The Warlords of Washington* (New York, 1948); Richard Polenberg, *War and Society: The United States, 1941–1945* (Philadelphia, 1972); John Morton Blum, *V Was for Victory* (New York, 1976); and Conrad C. Crane, *Bombs, Cities, and Civilians* (Lawrence, Kan., 1993).

For the industry's financial and business risks and labor relations, see Lynn Bollinger and Tom Lilley, *The Financial Position of the Aircraft Industry* (Cambridge, 1943), and Jacob Vander Meulen, *The Politics of Aircraft* (Lawrence, Kan., 1991). For an original source of B-29 data, see "B-29 Airframe and Components," August 28, 1944, Box 689, 452.1, Classified, Bulky, AAG 1942–1944. *New York Times* editors called the B-29 program the "greatest single undertaking" in industrial history in their issue for December 11, 1944.

On wartime aircraft production see A. B. Berghell, *Production Engineering in the Aircraft Industry* (Cambridge, Mass., 1944); F. D. Klein, *Process Practices in the Aircraft Industry* (New York, 1942); Tom Lilley et al., *Problems of Accelerating Aircraft Production during World War II* (Boston, 1947). On the production consortium used by aircraft companies to build B-29s see Mac Short "BDV Production of Flying Fortresses,"

Automotive and Aviation Industries, October 15, 1943. On the B-29 Committee see boxes 110 and 111 at the St. Louis Federal Records Center, especially "Organizations and Functions of the B-29 Committee," January 7, 1944, in Box 110. " . . . best results are secured . . . when there is a minimum of domination by the Army" is from a memo by Col. Orval Cook, Chief, Production Division, Matériel Command, Wright Field, Dayton, Ohio, August 25, 1943, in Box 111. On ill feelings among the B-29 manufacturers see the telephone transcript between A. G. Fisher and Gen. K. B. Wolfe for March 11 and December 8, 1943, Box 110. On the GM–Fisher works in Cleveland see Plancor 834, Box 353, Records of the Defense Plant Corporation, Record Group 234, National Archives.

For the hundreds of companies involved with the B-29 see "B-29 Contractors and Sub-Contractors," K168.3-82, Simpson Center, Maxwell AFB. On the complications and delays of B-29 modification see also at the Simpson Center Charles M. Thomas, "The Modification of Aircraft: Procedures, Policies, and Problems," May 22, 1945, K201-4; "Historical Supplement—Office of the AAF Plant Representative, Birmingham Modification Center, Alabama," January–March 1945, K208-2; Capt. Robert S. McNamara, Air Corp Statistical Office, "B-29 Status of Equipment," February 8, 1944, K761.3082; R. H. McDonough, "History of Supply, Maintenance and Training for the B-29," January 1946, K201-43. At the St. Louis Federal Records Center see "Difficulties Encountered in Manufacture of B-29 Airplanes," February 1944, Box 116, 06-15-04-9; "Status of the B-29 Project," January 9, 1944, Box 716, 004, Classified, in AAG Records for 1942–44. Also on Bechtel-McCone-Parsons–Birmingham, see Plancor 1548, Box 549, Records of the Defense Plant Corporation.

Many of the answers to the question of Why Wichita? may be found in the microfilmed newspapers and aviation files at the Wichita Public Library. See especially the *Wichita Eagle*, November 11, 1937, July 30, 1939, August 17 and September 22, 1940, March 26, 1942, and August 18 and 30, 1942; and the *Wichita Beacon*, April 29 and August 1, 1940, April 15, 1941, March 2, 1942, and August 17 and 29, 1945. See also the wartime plant newspaper *Boeing Plane Talk*.

A lively contemporary account is Shelby Cullom Davis, "Wichita Boom Town," *Current History*, January 10, 1941. According to government officials, Wichita was ideal because "the country is level, the climate ideal for flying and testing." For them Kansas was a "continuous landing field." See Plancor 139/140, Box 77, Records of the Defense Plant Corporation; "Overall Cost of Facilities, Wichita," Philip G. Johnson, president of the Boeing Company, to Undersecretary of War Robert Patterson, February 9,

1942, in "Emergency Plant Facilities" Box 71, 004.4, Unclassified; "Amortization of Facilities, Boeing Aircraft, Wichita Division," Box 31, 004, Unclassified, in AAG Records, 1940–42.

For important studies of how World War II affected the lives of American women see Gregory Chester, *Women in Defense Work during World War II* (New York, 1974); Sheena Gluck, *Rosie the Riveter Revisited: Women, the War, and Social Change* (Boston, 1982); D'Ann Campbell, *Women at War with America: Private Lives in a Patriotic Era* (Cambridge, Mass., 1984); Susan Hartmann, *The Homefront and Beyond: American Women in the 1940s* (Boston, 1982); Ruth Milkman, *Gender at Work: The Dynamics of Job Segregation by Sex during World War II* (Chicago, 1987). On women in the aircraft industry and at Wichita see Judith R. Johnson. "Uncle Sam Wanted Them Too! Women Aircraft Workers in Wichita during World War II," *Kansas History,* no. 1 (1994), and Jane Rhodes, "Women in the Aircraft Industry during World War II," *The Territorial,* May 1990.

A good sense of the attitudes of aircraft executives toward unions may be found in ACC 32.02.5, J. E. Schaefer, general manager of the Boeing–Wichita works, to James Murray, Boeing vice-president, December 24, 1940, in Reel 32.02.5, Records of the Aerospace Industries Association, National Air and Space Museum. For Larry Bell's involvement in the President's Employer Labor Conference see Reel 30.01.8.

On the Boeing operations in Seattle and Renton see the files in K202.2-52 at the Simpson Center, especially "Boeing Airplane Company— Seattle," January 9, 1943; "Case History of Boeing Aircraft Company Renton, Washington," May 1947, and "Special Inspection of the Administration of Cost-Plus-a-Fixed-Fee Contracts at the Seattle and Renton Plants of the Boeing Aircraft Company," November 6, 1942. See also "Boeing Aircraft Company," August 26, 1944, Box 101, in the Records of Robert A. Lovett, Assistant Secretary of War for Air, Record Group 107, National Archives; and Plancor 156, Boxes 91 and 92, Records of the Defense Plant Corporation.

"In view of the confusion at Boeing-Renton . . . " is in "Appraisal of B-29 Production, Modification and Availability," October 12, 1944, Box 719, 452.1, Classified, AAG Records 1942–44. For details of Boeing's relations with its workers see the Records of the International Association of Machinists, President's Files, reels 32, 33, 329, 355, at the State Historical Society of Wisconsin in Madison.

For material on B-29 production in Omaha see George A. Larson, "Nebraska's World War II Bomber Plant: The Glenn L. Martin-Nebraska Company," *Nebraska History,* Spring 1993; "History of the Glenn L.

Martin–Nebraska Company," unpublished manuscript, and "The Glenn L. Martin–Nebraska Company Employment Summary, Entire Facility as of January 5, 1945," both in the Glenn L. Martin Papers, State Archives, Nebraska State Historical Society, Lincoln. See also Jerold Simmons, "Public Leadership in a World War II Boom Town: Bellevue, Nebraska," *Nebraska History* (Winter 1984); V. Kastens, A Survey of the Employment Situation in Omaha, Nebraska, Nebraska State Employment Service, for the NDAC (January 1941).

The Sarpy County Museum has copies of the company newspaper, the *Martin Star,* and "History of Building D," Offutt Air Force Base pamphlet 210-1. See also the *Omaha World Herald,* "Cut Red Tape," December 27, 1940; "They're Out to Beat Hitler," July 20, 1941, "Women Workers at Bomber Plant," December 13, 1942, and the Omaha Chamber of Commerce Journal, for December 1940 and March 1941 in the Omaha Public Library, Reference Department.

On major subassemblers' distrust of their contracts with the primes and their call for direct contracts with the federal government and for "these lawyers," see Orval Cook to Chief of the Production Division, Wright Field, September 6, 1943, and telephone typescript for October 9, 1943, in Box 111, St. Louis Records Center. See also "Fort Crook Project" documents in boxes 58 and 116, Lovett Records, "Military Investigations," Box 268, 333.5, Classified, Bulky, AAG 1942–44.

Because the Bell–Marietta plant was so problematic it left a large body of government records. See A. O. Willauer, "Outline History of the B-29 Program at the Bell Bomber Plant"; "Historical Report, 1 April–30 June 1945, of the AAF Plant Representative, Marietta Aircraft Assembly Plant," K208-1, Simpson Research Center. On Bell's lofting see Capt. H. L. Webster, B-29 Coordinator, to General Echols, April 7, 1943, Box 111; "We're forty miles from nowhere" complained Larry Bell in a phone call with Colonel Cook on October 2, 1943, Box 111; "hacked out the first article," General Wolfe to Colonel Cook, November 3, 1943, Box 116, all in the St. Louis Records Center.

For workforce shortages at Bell see P. Castigny, War Manpower Commission, Atlanta, to Earle Cook, Vice President, Fulton National Bank, September 2, 1943, Box 38, 004.02, Unclassified, AAG 1942–44; "Labor Market Survey of Marietta, Georgia Area," January 1, 1943, Box 18, Entry 21, and "Information on the Atlanta-Marietta Area," Box 2, Entry 17, War Manpower Commission Records, Region VII, Record Group 211; and documents in Box 2, Records of the Fair Employment Practices Commission, Record Group 228, all at the National Archives, Atlanta Branch.

See Larry Bell to General Arnold, February 19, 1944, Box 523, 452.1,

NOTE ON SOURCES

103

Classified, Bulky, AAG 1945, and minutes for February 14 and 21, April 18, July 3, and October 26, 1944, Aircraft Production Board, 334, Classified, Bulky, Box 334, AAG 1942–44. See also documents in Box 717, 452.1, Classified, AAG 1942–44. For complaints from locals about mismanagement at Marietta see Box 685, Records of the Truman Committee, Record Group 46, National Archives.

The *New York Times* followed the Marietta Project. See the issues for February 23, 1942, March 13, 14, 15, July 14, and November 4, 1943, as well as regular news stories and features in the *Atlanta Constitution* and *Journal*.

On who built the engines see the vertical file "Wright 3350" and the company newspaper "Wright at the Moment" in the Archives and Library of the National Air and Space Museum. For material on Curtiss-Wright's relations with its workers see the Records of the Machinists, reels 341 and 342. Important documents on Wright-Woodridge are in Plancor 994,

Box 403, Records of the Defense Plant Corporation; boxes 101, 141, 160, Lovett Records; Box 29, .004, Classified, AAG 1942–44. For studies and criticisms of Curtiss-Wright's top management and military investigations of Wright-Woodridge and Dodge-Chicago see boxes 101, 160, 141, Lovett Records, and boxes 140, 141, 142 of Undersecretary of War Robert P. Patterson Papers at the Library of Congress. For Chrysler-Dodge and the R-3350 in Chicago see Box 22, .004, Bulky, Classified, AAG 1942–44, and Box 112, St. Louis Federal Record Center. See also Plancor 792, Box 438, Records of the Defense Plant Corporation, and a large report by the Bureau of Manpower Utilization of the War Manpower Commission, Box 4, Entry 217, Record Group 211.

For a military cost-benefit assessment of the B-29 program see W. B. Shockley, "A Quantitative Appraisal of Some Phases of the B-29 Program," May 1, 1945, for Edward Bowles, Box 233, 452.01, Classified, AAG 1945.